T0298855

THE STATE OF POVERTY AND FOOD INSECURITY IN MASERU, LESOTHO

RESETSELEMANG LEDUKA, JONATHAN CRUSH,
BRUCE FRAYNE, CAMERON MCCORDIC,
THOPE MATOBO, TS'EPISO E. MAKOA,
MATSELISO MPHALE, MMANTAI PHAILA
AND MOIPONE LETSIE

SERIES EDITOR: PROF. JONATHAN CRUSH

© AFSUN 2015

Published by the African Food Security Urban Network (AFSUN)
African Centre for Cities, University of Cape Town, Private Bag X3
Rondebosch 7701, South Africa
www.afsun.org

First published 2015

ISBN 978-1-920597-12-2

Cover photo of Maseru by Jonathan Crush

Production by Bronwen Dachs Müller, Cape Town

Printed by MegaDigital, Cape Town

Contents

Tables

FIGURES

Previous Publications in the AFSUN Series

1. INTRODUCTION

Lesotho regularly features in the African and international media as a country blighted by drought, hunger and food insecurity.[1] Much of the discussion about the causes and remedies for food insecurity, including within Lesotho itself, focuses on the rural population and the precipitous decline in domestic food production in recent decades. The IFRC, for example, recently argued that "persistent food insecurity continues to be a chronic problem in Lesotho and a key obstacle in the country's development agenda. The food crisis has been amplified due to the existence of a number of interlinking issues including periodic droughts which have led to crop failures, excessive soil erosion, declining rangeland conditions, chronic poverty and the effects of HIV on the labour force."[2] In August 2012, the Lesotho Prime Minister, Motsoahae Thomas Thabane, declared a food security state of emergency in Lesotho.[3] As well as calling for increased food aid, he proposed several emergency responses including (a) implementing the National Strategic Development Plan in which agriculture is one of the key strategies; (b) improving agricultural productivity and food security through maximum use of arable land, subsidized inputs and promotion of drought-resistant crops; (c) scaling up conservation farming and homestead farming/gardening; and (d) promoting nutrition services to pregnant women and mothers. Since food security planning and response is the line responsibility of the Lesotho Department of Agriculture and Food Security, it is perhaps not surprising that food insecurity is viewed exclusively as a rural problem and that the proposed solutions all focused on smallholder farmers and rural development. This tendency is perpetuated and reproduced by most of the multilateral and bilateral donors who have set up shop in Lesotho.

While it is undeniable that food insecurity is an endemic problem in Lesotho's rural villages, the rural bias of both donors and government ignores the fact that poverty and food insecurity are increasingly important urban issues as well.[4] Lesotho certainly does not have the mega-cities with millions of residents that are increasingly characteristic of African urbanization. However, it is urbanizing at a rapid rate and this reality needs to be acknowledged, understood and planned for in food security discussions and debates. With the exception of one seminal report by the LVAC/WFP in 2008, there has been little attention paid to the drivers, prevalence and characteristics of food insecurity in Lesotho's urban centres.[5] This report aims to raise the profile of what must inevitably become an increasingly important challenge and one, furthermore, which cannot be handled by the Ministry of Agriculture and Food Security on its own or the myriad donors and experts who continue to see Lesotho as a pre-modern rural society.

This report is the latest in a series on Southern African cities issued by AFSUN. Like the previous reports, it focuses on one city (Maseru) and on poor neighbourhoods and households in that city. The AFSUN Urban Food Security Baseline Survey, on which this report is based, was implemented in Maseru in late 2008. The findings are still relevant to contemporary Lesotho for the following reasons: (a) there is no evidence that the urban food security situation has improved in the intervening years and there are strong reasons for thinking it has deteriorated; food imports are up, remittances from South Africa are down and employment in Maseru's garment factories has been declining; (b) the AFSUN survey was undertaken towards the end of the global and regional food price crisis of 2007-2008, which had a strong negative impact on the food security of poor urban populations. An analysis of what this meant for households in Lesotho is imperative since food price increases and dramatic spikes are certainly not a thing of the past and need to be planned for; and (c) by drawing attention to the nature and magnitude of urban food security in Lesotho's capital, this study can contribute to the reformulation of food security policy in the country as both a rural and urban issue and as both a food production and access issue.

This report is divided into several sections. The first describes the course and trajectory of urbanization in Lesotho and the morphology of Maseru in order to demonstrate that rapid urban growth is a reality that needs greater research and policy attention. The next section examines the state of food production in Lesotho and the various explanations advanced regarding the ongoing decline of domestic agriculture. The report concurs with the argument that farming is simply one of a number of livelihood strategies pursued by rural households and not necessarily the most important. As a result, overall production in the country continues to decline and food imports from neighbouring South Africa to increase. The third section of the report examines the determinants and dimensions of the 2007-2008 global food price crisis and its local manifestations as background to a consideration of the impact of the crisis on urban households in Maseru. The report then presents and discusses the results of the AFSUN baseline food security survey in Maseru, demonstrating that the urban poor in that city are amongst the most food insecure in the entire region. The conclusion argues for a reorientation of discussions of food security in Lesotho away from the longstanding obsession with rural development and domestic agricultural production towards more emphasis on questions of food accessibility, and includes suggestions for a new integrated approach to policy-making on urban food insecurity.

2. URBANIZATION IN LESOTHO

Lesotho has traditionally been portrayed as an impoverished rural island that acts primarily as a labour reserve for South Africa.[6] This dated picture does little justice to the transformation that has taken place in recent decades. Like most other African countries, Lesotho is experiencing a rapid urban transition with large-scale internal migration to the urban centres, higher urban than rural population growth rates, and depopulation of the more remote mountainous areas of the country. The urban population comprised just over 7% of the total at independence in 1966.[7] By 1976, this had increased to 10% and to 24% in 2006 (Table 1). The absolute number of urban dwellers increased from 127,000 in 1976 to 444,000 in 2006. The UN projects that urbanization in Lesotho will rise to 39% by 2025 and to 58% by 2050.[8] Most of the country's population live in villages in the lowlands of the country and no one in these areas is more than an hour or two from the nearest urban centre. Thus, even the country's "rural" people regularly visit the urban centres and have their lives and livelihoods framed by what goes on there.

TABLE 1: Population Indicators in Lesotho, 1976-2006				
	1976	1986	1996	2006
Total population	1,216,815	1,606,000	1,841,967	1,872,721
Urban population	127,435	188,028	312,444	444,541
Urban as % of total population	10.5	11.8	16.9	23.7
Maseru population	65,031	98,017	137,837	227,880
Maseru as % of total population	5.3	6.1	7.5	12.2
Maseru growth rate	6.6%	5.9%	3.5%	5.2%
Source: Bureau of Statistics Census Reports				

Maseru, the capital of Lesotho, is the country's largest city and is located just across the Caledon (Mohokare) River from neighbouring South Africa. It was originally established as a police camp on the eastern side of the river after the 1869 Treaty of Aliwal North between the British and the Boer Republic of the Orange Free State. During the colonial era that followed, this police camp assumed the semblance of a small town with the addition of commercial, educational and health functions.[9] Major shifts in the face of the city came with independence in 1966, including expanded government facilities, the in-migration of rural families with little prospect of deriving incomes from agriculture, and the expansion of socio-economic opportunities. As a result, by 1986, 60% of Lesotho's urban population lived in Maseru (Table 2). This dropped to 44% in 1996 as other urban centres (especially nearby Teyatayeneng) began to grow. However, with the growth of textile manufacturing in the 1990s, Maseru's primacy again become more pronounced. In 2006, 46% of the urban population lived there. The population of Maseru reached 228,000 that year, well in excess of Lesotho's other urban centres, none of which had a population of over 80,000. Until 1980, the urban boundary was no more than 3km from the city centre. However, the extension of urban boundaries to enclose unplanned peri-urban areas effectively expanded the urban area from 23km² to 143km².[10] On average, the household density in Maseru is 41 households per hectare.[11]

TABLE 2: Population of Urban Centres in Lesotho, 1976-2006								
Urban Area	1976	%	1986	%	1996	%	2006	%
Butha-Buthe	7,740	6.4	8,340	4.6	12,610	4.0	14,070	3.3
Hlotse	6,300	5.4	8,080	4.4	23,120	7.4	55,180	13.1
Maputsoe	15,820	13.6	11,200	6.1	27,950	9.0	–	–
Teyateyaneng	8,590	7.4	12,930	7.1	48,870	15.6	61,270	14.5
Maseru	55,030	47.2	109,200	59.6	137,840	44.1	195,300	46.3
Mafeteng	8,200	7.1	12,180	6.6	20,800	6.7	31,760	7.5
Mohale's Hoek	5,200	4.5	7,900	4.3	17,870	5.7	27,690	6.6
Quithing (Moyeni)	3,500	3.0	4,310	2.3	9,860	3.2	13,490	3.2
Qacha's Nek	4,840	4.1	4,600	2.5	4,800	1.5	8,100	1.9
Mokhotlong	1,480	1.3	2,390	1.3	4,270	1.4	8,490	2.0
Thaba-Tseka	–	–	2,150	1.2	4,450	1.4	6,750	1.6
Total	116,620	100	183,200	100	312,440	100	422,100	100
Source: Leduka (2012: 4)								

Rapid urbanization in Lesotho is driven by a combination of natural increase and internal migration. For example, only 32% of the population of Maseru have lived in the city since birth (Figure 1). In absolute terms, this means that only around 70,000 of the city's residents were born in Maseru. As many as 36% moved there between 2007 and 2011. Of the remainder, 12% have lived in the city for 5-9 years and 11% for 11-19 years. Long-term migrants (who have lived in the city for more than 20 years) make up only 9% of the population. Only Thaba-Tseka and Qacha's Nek, amongst Lesotho's urban centres, have a lower proportion of locally-born and a higher proportion of recent migrants.

Spatially, Maseru has a linear central area, with middle and high-income housing along its length, but especially in the area known as CBD West. The residential parts of CBD West are largely inhabited by professional and administrative categories of civil servants, wealthy citizens and expatriates. CBD West is the most upmarket part of central Maseru, with high-rise office complexes, department stores, hotels and malls. Informal-sector activities are rarely found in CBD West because of heavy polic-ing.[12] In CBD East, the urban character is more congested and less formal. The main bus and taxi terminus is located there, as well as informal and municipal markets. The area is a lively mix of formal and informal busi-nesses that cater mostly for people with low incomes. Virtually all the street and alleyway spaces are taken up by informal traders selling fruit, vegetables and other food, as well as clothing and household items.

FIGURE 1: Length of Residence in Maseru, 2011

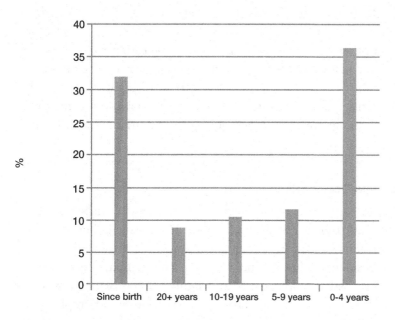

Source: LDS (2013)

Maseru's outlying residential areas have limited commercial development except for various small, unauthorized shopping centres that are springing up along the main arterial roads leading out of the city. Informal street traders are increasing in numbers here in response to the intolerance of street trading by local authorities in inner–city locations.[13] As Maseru has expanded, it has incorporated traditional villages. As a result, modern and customary laws are applied side by side. However, a few traditional villages have remained distinct and are characterized by dilapidated housing and poverty. Similarly, the CBD is not fully integrated with the peri-urban areas in terms of service provision, with the latter areas remaining largely under-served. Recent attempts by government and parastatals to develop residential areas for different income groups have not been very success-ful since these institutions only sell sites and have no capacity to control what happens on them and to provide infrastructure services. However, the rest of the city, and particularly the unplanned urban sprawl that has developed on farmlands around traditional villages, exhibits high levels of social integration where the rich and the poor live side by side. The World Food Programme estimates that 94% of Maseru households have access to piped or protected well water and 96% to flush toilets, suggesting that Maseru has benefited from being the largest urban centre in Lesotho with extensive investment in basic urban services in recent years.[14]

A substantial proportion of the urban population lives in rented accommodation, which has been a lucrative investment for a significant number of households in Maseru. This is directly attributable to the growth of the garment manufacturing industry in the last 20 years. Many factory workers, and other low-paid public and private sector employees, live in rental housing consisting of rows of single and double rooms (colloquially known as *maline* in Lesotho). In both Maseru and Maputsoe, where the garment factories are concentrated, *maline* have arguably eased the pressure on the public sector to provide housing for the urban poor (Box 1).

BOX 1: *Maline* Occupants in Maseru

The Regulatory Framework Survey conducted by Sechaba Consultants in 2001 visited 309 households in Ha Tsolo and Ha Thetsane. The households were chosen at random, and thus include old and new residents. The area includes many of the textile factories that have provided employment to roughly 50,000 workers over the past several years. Many textile workers have found employment in these factories, and thus have found accommodation near work. Nearly 66% were classified as poor or destitute, compared to 34% who were classified as of average and above average wealth. In contrast, relatively fewer non-migrants were found to be destitute or poor, while a relatively higher proportion of this latter group was found to be of average and above average wealth. In brief, migrants in Ha Tsolo and Ha Thetsane were generally poorer than those who were born in Maseru. The residents are representative of the people newly arriving in Maseru in order to find industrial work. Seventy-two percent of the households in the Ha Tsolo/ Ha Thetsane sample are renting their houses at the moment, as opposed to 23% overall for Maseru in the poverty study of 1999. Those who moved to the Ha Tsolo/Ha Thetsane area before 1998 are far more likely to own their property (58%) than those who moved in 1998 or after (14%). Ha Tsolo and Ha Thetsane attract people who are willing to pay high rents for sub-standard housing, because transport costs from more distant locations would eat up at least one-third of a monthly wage. It is mostly women in these *maline* who find jobs. Male relatives of these women thus are forced into gender-reversal roles. They must clean the house, take care of children, and sit at home while the woman goes to work.

Source: J. Gay and C. Leduka, "Migration and Urban Governance in Southern Africa: The Case of Maseru" Paper presented at the SAMP/COJ/SACN/MDP Workshop on Migration and Urban Governance: Building Inclusive Cities in the SADC, Johannesburg, 2005, pp. 25-6.

FIGURE 2: Structure of Maseru City

Source: Google Maps, 2014

Climate and geography have played a role in driving urban growth in Lesotho. Most of the country is mountainous, receives variable rainfall and is susceptible to erosion and frost, creating unsuitable conditions for agricultural production.[15] In areas where crop cultivation is possible, yields are low and unpredictable leading to extreme vulnerability to food insecurity.[16] As a result, the overcrowded lowlands, where most of the urban population resides, attract people from rural households in the Lesotho highlands and other impoverished rural areas in search of employment opportunities.[17] Overall, Lesotho's rapid urbanization is evidence of an ongoing shift in household livelihoods away from agriculture and towards wage employment within and outside the country.[18]

3. EXPLAINING DECLINING FOOD PRODUCTION

Despite the well-intentioned efforts of generations of rural development experts, Lesotho is not food self-sufficient. The three main crops grown by smallholders are maize, wheat and sorghum. Together they cover 85% of the cultivated area of the country with maize predominant (62%) followed by sorghum (14%) and wheat (9%).[19] Other cultivars include beans, potatoes and peas. Due to the mountainous conditions in most of the country, the limited availability of arable land and the variability of rainfall, only the northwestern area of the country is really suitable for maize production (Figure 3).[20] The area sown with cereals has declined steadily since independence from 450,000 hectares in 1960 to 150,000 hectares in 2006. Total cereal production has also declined over time. Before 1980 (with the exception of drought years), total grain production was 200-250,000 tonnes per year (Figure 4). In 1996, total production spiked at 274,000 tonnes and fell year-on-year over the next decade to 126,00 tonnes in 2006 and only 72,000 tonnes in 2007 (a drought year).[21]

Maize, sorghum and wheat make up three-quarters of the country's agricultural production in the average year but contribute only 30% of domestic requirements. Few rural, and no urban, households are self-sufficient, necessitating food purchase to meet household needs. Studies in rural Lesotho demonstrate that marginalized households in all areas of the country are extremely vulnerable to food insecurity and dependent on food purchase for survival.[22] Households in the mountainous areas of Lesotho are especially vulnerable to staple food shortages due to their inability to produce much food and their limited access to markets.[23] In the market, whole grain maize is supplied predominantly by domestic producers while maize meal is imported from South Africa. A national survey in 2010-2011 found that only 8% of agricultural households sold any of their produce (although the authors attribute what they see as a surprisingly low figure to extensive crop loss through flooding).[24] In 2009, maize meal, wheat flour and other milled products to the value of

LSL318 million (about USD27 million) were imported, primarily from South Africa.[25] Paradoxically, domestic whole grain maize tends to be more expensive than imported maize meal.[26] The amount of imported grain varies, depending on domestic consumption and relative prices. In the early 1980s, grain imports reached an all-time high and made up 40-60% of annual consumption. Imports dropped in the late 1980s and 1990s but after 2000 began to rise rapidly, making up around two-thirds of overall consumption. In 2011/12, the most recent year for which data is available, the domestic cereal requirement for maize, sorghum and wheat was 360,000 tonnes of which only 83,000 tonnes was available locally (through production and storage carry-over).[27] Projected imports included 135,000 tonnes of maize and 164,000 tonnes of wheat.

FIGURE 3: Lesotho Areas Suitable for Maize Production

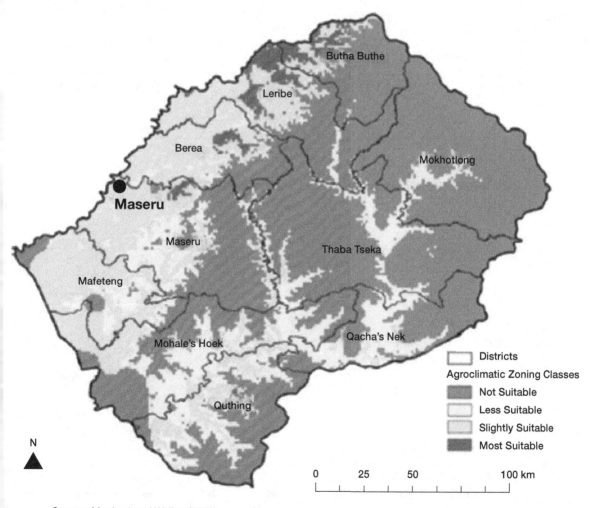

Source: Moeletsi and Walker (2013)

FIGURE 4: Cereal Production in Lesotho, 1960-2012

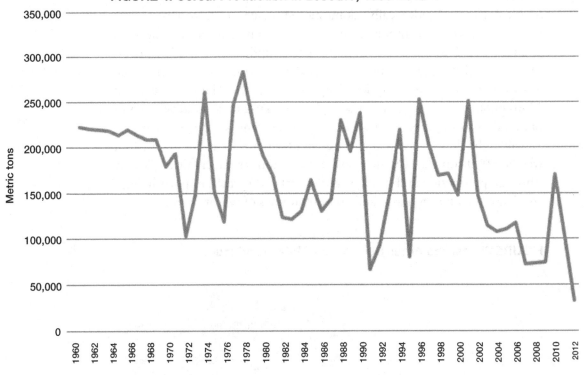

Source: World Bank, 2014

FIGURE 5: Grain Imports into Lesotho, 1961-2010

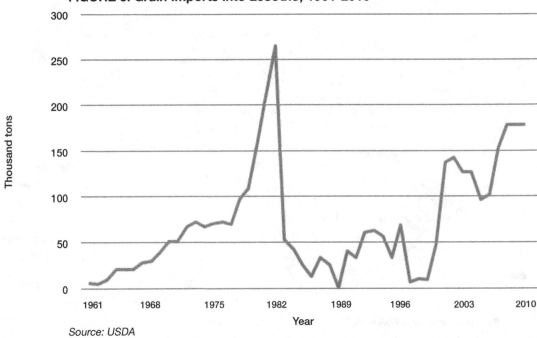

Source: USDA

Various reasons have been advanced for the ongoing decline in agricultural production in Lesotho. These can be distilled into four main types of explanation: technological, market-based, health-related and environmental. In terms of technological arguments, it is often pointed out that only 10% of the land area is suitable for agricultural development.[28] As a result, arable land is at a premium and competition for it has increased with population growth. The area of arable land per person in Lesotho declined from 0.4 hectares in 1961 to 0.2 hectares in 2008.[29] One author suggests that there is also an annual loss of 1,000 hectares of arable land due to erosion.[30] As a result, securing access to arable land for crop production is difficult and expensive. Lesotho's land tenure system is blamed for constraining the emergence of larger, economically-viable farms.[31] Also, the persistence of traditional agricultural practices is viewed by the World Bank as a cause of low productivity and declining production.[32] The Famine Early Warning Systems Network (FEWSNET) points to the loss of labour "due to HIV/AIDS; population pressure on land size with ineffective agricultural extension to manage environmental constraints; constraints to input access; and the impact of livestock theft on the availability of draught power."[33] Another recent analysis of the prospects for horticulture in Lesotho blames "soil erosion, poor agricultural practices, frequent droughts, increased cost of farming inputs and relative openness to external influences."[34]

A market-based argument mainly associated with the World Bank is that the decline in production is due to the limited capacity of Basotho producers to compete with cheaper imported food. The costs associated with land tenure and the challenges faced by agricultural producers place pressures on the price of domestically-produced food, limiting the viability of agriculture as an income-producing strategy. FEWSNET argues that maize seed and fertilizer cost significantly more in Lesotho than in South Africa, where maize is produced on large, highly-mechanized commercial farms.[35] The country's poor transportation infrastructure does not connect producers to urban markets.[36] Despite all this, donors and international agencies, including the World Bank, continue to believe in a commercial future for Lesotho agriculture provided that an enabling environment for agribusiness can be created:

> To date the participation of the private sector has been only marginal. The private sector provides little market access for farmers; remains inert with respect to technology choices; conforms grudgingly to regulations even when these make little economic sense; and in selective sectors where growth prospects were once attractive remains passive while asset values erode and regulatory institutions diminish in their capacities. The private sector provides little capital, assumes minimal

performance risk within the sector and demonstrates little strategic initiative. Within the Lesotho agricultural system, farmers themselves have been subordinated as welfare recipients. Their ranks are dominated by small-scale sharecroppers and small-scale landholders, which are organized only at the household level. Farmers have become passive receivers of technical advice, beneficiaries of public sector subsidized inputs and price takers in local markets, which are particularly volatile because of their small case and isolation from other markets. No effective cooperative or association system operates within the agricultural sector.[37]

A third common explanation for the decline is health-related and reflects the impact of HIV and AIDS on rural communities and smallholder agriculture. Lesotho has one of the world's highest rates of HIV.[38] The spread of HIV among rural food-producing households can lead to decreased agricultural productivity due to labour shortages, the burden of caring for family members with AIDS, and the loss of farming skills and assets.[39] Access to healthcare services in Lesotho has been challenged by limited infrastructure available for service provision and limited government capacity to support public health initiatives.[40]

A final set of explanations for agricultural decline focuses on the impact of environmental change. Clearly, as in 2002, 2007 and 2012, extreme weather events can play havoc with harvests. But this does not necessarily explain the overall downward trend in agricultural production. Nevertheless, researchers and international agencies increasingly see these events as symptomatic of climate change. The UNEP, for example, argues that Lesotho is "one of the countries highly vulnerable to the impact of climate change, deserving special attention. The country experiences frequent droughts that result in poor harvests and large livestock losses to rural farmers, exacerbating poverty and suffering. Heavy snowfalls, strong winds and floods that pose devastating social impacts also affect Lesotho. These adverse climatic conditions undermine the economic development of the country and the well-being of the nation."[41] UNICEF draws an even closer connection: climatic changes "have contributed to reduced crop yields around the country. Without enough means to make a living or grow their own food, many families cannot afford the cost of food, leaving them food insecure. As a result, many children in Lesotho suffer from malnutrition."[42] Lesotho's National Adaptation Plan of Action devotes most of its attention to interventions in the rural farming sector. The hard evidence for links between climate change and agricultural decline is currently limited to climate and crop yield modelling[43] and studies of individual case study villages.[44] Climate change is increasingly seen as a contributing factor to agricultural decline.[45] Ironically, the International

Food Policy Research Institute (IFPRI) suggests that climate change in Lesotho is grounds for optimism: "the area planted to maize will remain more or less unchanged, but production and yields will increase by more than 200 percent between 2010 and 2050. Production, yields, and harvested area for sorghum are also expected to increase substantially."[46]

Perhaps the most penetrating multi-causal analysis of the reason for agricultural decline comes from a long-time observer of rural social and economic transformation in Lesotho, Steven Turner, who reinstates human agency into the equation and argues that Basotho households are not driven by immutable structural or environmental forces but make choices about where to put their limited energies and resources:

> Agriculture as it is practised today in Lesotho can most usefully be understood as part of a larger portfolio of livelihood options open to Basotho households. As a consequence, agriculture has moved further and further from a business undertaking and increasingly toward a mode of social security. In the process Basotho farm families have become increasingly passive in coping with their dwindling resource base. Growing numbers of lowland field owners have done their sums and decided that this kind of production is too risky to continue. More and more land in this zone lies fallow, which may at least have some environmental benefits (although it upsets those who believe that the country can and should produce more grain).... One of the many paradoxes in Lesotho agriculture is farmers' (addiction to maize) and their determination to grow such a challenging crop. Despite the introduction of early-maturing varieties that have largely replaced wheat and peas in the mountains, and despite modern Basotho's dietary preference for it, maize is not a very suitable grain crop for Lesotho.[47]

Lesotho is, and will continue to be, heavily dependent on food imports from South Africa. The only real question in the long-term, especially in urban areas like Maseru, is how to make that food affordable and accessible.

4. RELIANCE ON FOOD IMPORTS

Cereal import dependency can be defined by the national ratio of cereal imports over the sum of cereal production and the difference between cereal imports and exports (Figure 5). Domestic food price index scores are determined by dividing food Purchasing Power Parity (PPP) by the general PPP in the country, while domestic food price volatility is defined by the standard deviation of the food price index over the previous five years.[48] Two interesting trends can be observed. First, the liberalization of the Lesotho food market in 1997 was followed by decreased food price volatility and a continued decrease in domestic food prices. Second, while domestic food prices have continued to fall, domestic food price volatility has distributed around 20 standard deviations and appears to approximately track with cereal import dependency.[49] These observations demonstrate the vulnerability of the Lesotho food market to international food price volatility in spite of a long term overall reduction in domestic food prices. While importing food has resulted in steadily decreasing food prices over the past few decades, the country remains susceptible to food price volatility on the regional and international market.

FIGURE 6: Cereal Import Dependence, Food Price and Food Price Volatility in Lesotho, 1996-2008

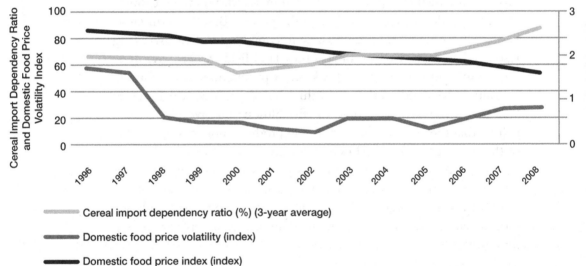

Cereal import dependency ratio (%) (3-year average)

Domestic food price volatility (index)

Domestic food price index (index)

Source: FAO (2012)

Lesotho is surrounded by South Africa and highly integrated into its economy. Both countries belong to the South African Customs Union and the Rand Monetary Area. Lesotho's currency is fixed to the South African rand. In 2011, 96% of Lesotho's LSL10.6 million in imports were from South Africa.[50] Table 3 shows the relative importance of different types of food import. The vast majority of imports by value are processed foods from South Africa including wheat flour, maize meal, oils and fats, beverages, sugar, baked goods, dairy, pasta and canned goods. While fresh meat is also imported in relatively large quantities, imports of fresh fruit and vegetables are relatively low. Heavy dependence on imports from South Africa for virtually all fresh and processed foodstuffs makes the average urban household in Lesotho extremely vulnerable to food price shocks. This was especially evident during the global food price crisis of 2007-2008.

TABLE 3: Value of Food Imports into Lesotho, 2011	
	Value of imports (LSL million)
Milled products (flour, meal)	318,043
Meat and offal	280,867
Processed oils and fats	218,646
Beverages (alcoholic and non-alcoholic)	203,932
Cereals	160,684
Sugar and sugar products	154,588
Processed baked goods	145,304
Dairy products	130,376
Processed cereal products, pasta	124,144
Processed fruit and vegetables	64,319
Coffee, tea, spices	54,048
Vegetables	52,219
Processed meat and fish	51,235
Fruits	19,061
Live animals	18,513
Fish and seafood	8,020

5. THE 2007–2008 FOOD PRICE CRISIS

In 2008, after decades of relative food price stability, food prices on international markets rose by 36% in only a year. The sharp rise in the price of staples such as wheat, maize, and rice led to trade shocks (including sharp increases in international export quantities) in these markets in 2008, with knock-on shocks on other food commodities (Figure 6).[51] In the case of African nations, the transmission of this international food price volatility into domestic markets was mediated by domestic infrastructure and market access, and the degree of dependence on food imports.[52] Commodity imports thus play a determining role in the transmission of international food prices into domestic African markets. One study of domestic and international food prices among Sub-Saharan African nations between 2005 and 2008 reported a correlation of 0.73 among net food importing nations and only 0.54 among net food exporting nations.[53] In Southern and Eastern Africa, food products appear to be more susceptible to international price volatility than non-food products.[54] This is especially the case amongst staple foods like maize, the prices for which can remain volatile months after a trade shock.

FIGURE 7: Global Food Commodities Indices, 2000-2012

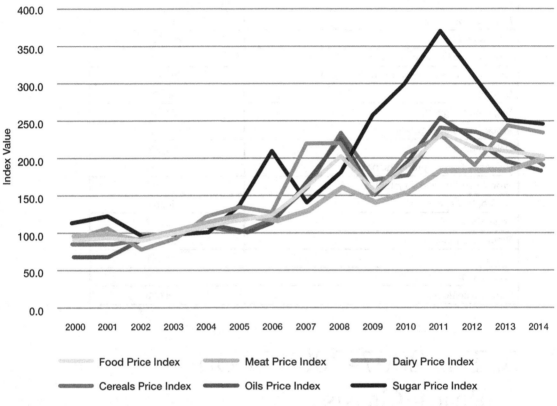

Source: FAO

Food price inflation peaked in South Africa at 18.5% in July 2008 and remained above 10% for the rest of 2008.[55] The price of maize meal (the primary staple for poor households) increased by 38% from March 2007 to June 2008.[56] The price of a loaf of white bread increased by 50% between April 2007 and December 2008.[57] Figures 6 and 7 show the dramatic price increases in wheat and bread in South Africa in 2007-2008. There is some debate in the literature about the nature of the relationship between global and South African food prices with one study claiming that although "external influences do matter, South African food price movements are mainly due to domestic influences."[58] Another found a strong correlation between international and South African prices.[59] Around 63% of the world price variation for maize meal is transmitted to the local retail price.[60] The figures for three main cereals were even higher: 98% for maize, 93% for wheat and 80% for rice.[61] The price of both global and South African maize increased in 2008 but peaked at different times with the latter peaking first (Figure 9). As Figure 10 shows there was a direct relationship between the rising global and South African price of rice (all of which is imported).

FIGURE 8: Spot Price for Wheat in South Africa, 2000-2010

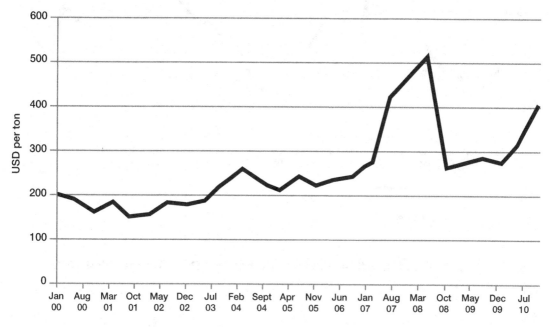

Source: Kirsten (2012)

FIGURE 9: Retail Prices of White and Brown Bread, South Africa, 2000-2010

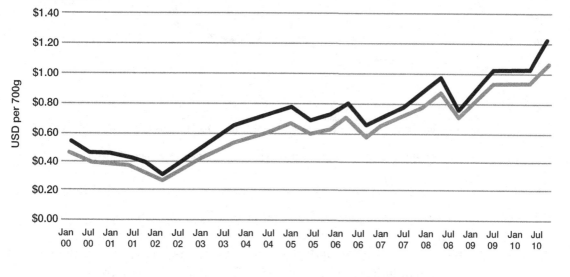

White Bread   Brown Bread

Source: Kirsten (2012)

FIGURE 10: South African and Global Maize Price Trends, 2000-2010

Source: Kirsten (2012)

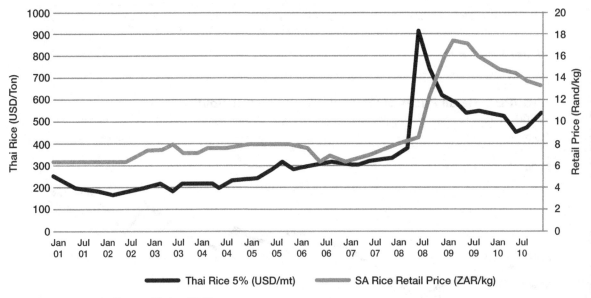

FIGURE 11: South African and Global Rice Price Trends, 2000-2010

Source: Kirsten (2012)

Given that the majority of food purchased in Lesotho is imported from South Africa, retail food prices are closely tied in the two countries, although one study found that Lesotho retailers changed food prices every 2.4 months on average between 2002 and 2009, compared to 5.9 months amongst South African retailers.[62] In a review of price inflation in Lesotho between 2003 and 2012, another study demonstrated that food price inflation spiked higher than non-food price inflation during the 2008 food price crisis although shocks in the price of non-food items also impacted on food prices (Figure 12).[63] Food prices also tend to be higher in urban than rural areas. The Central Bank of Lesotho suggested that food price inflation in 2007-2008 was caused by a combination of increased demand for grains on the international market and the impact of the 2007 drought.[64]

FIGURE 12: Food and Non-Food Inflation in Lesotho, 2003-2012 (%)

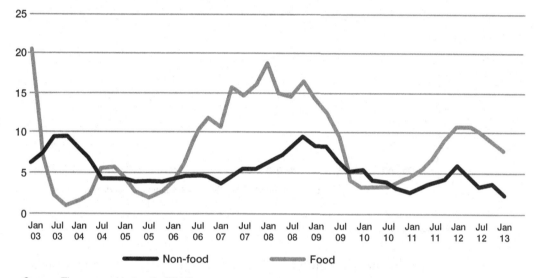

Source: Thamae and Letsoela (2014)

In South Africa (and by extension Lesotho) food price inflation between 2007 and 2009 disproportionately impacted on the poor. To buy the same food basket in 2008/9 as they had in 2007/8, the poorest households had to spend 13% more of their income (Figure 10). This proportion consistently declined with increased income to only 0.7% more of their income for those in the highest income group. General analyses of the food price crisis disagree on whether the rural or the urban poor were hardest hit.[65] Certainly, cities across the Global South exploded in food riots, which suggests intense levels of urban hardship and discontent.[66] In Southern Africa, Maputo was the only city to experience violent street protests.[67] Poor rural households, mostly scattered across the countryside or in small villages, would have found it difficult to mount similar large-scale protests. So the absence of food riots in the countryside cannot be taken as evidence that price increases has no impact on rural food security. In general, though, poor urban households that purchase most of their food, and where the majority of household income is spent on food, are inherently more likely to be negatively affected by price rises, with female-headed households at particular risk.[68]

FIGURE 13: Impact of Food Price Inflation by Income in South Africa, 2007/8-2008/9

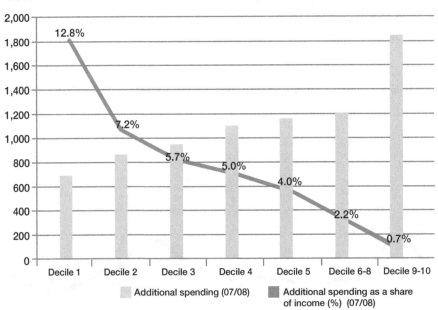

Source: Kirsten (2012)

One of the more insightful analyses of the specifically urban food security impacts of the 2007-2008 global food price crisis argues that "most policy prescriptions focused on addressing rural food production constraints, food stocks and macroeconomic measures. Action in these areas potentially contributes to longer-term urban food security, but policy makers and analysts paid less attention to direct improvements in urban food security."[69] Poor urban households tend to respond with a variety of coping strategies including going without meals, eating smaller quantities, reducing spending on other necessities and reducing their consumption of higher priced animal-source foods, fruits, vegetables and pulses in favour of cheaper, non-processed staples. They also "buy on credit, seek food from neighbours, rely on food programmes and adjust intra-household distribution." However, many poor urban households have "little room for manoeuvre."[70]

6. Survey Methodology

The Maseru food security baseline survey covered a sample of 800 house-holds drawn from two census urban constituencies (33 and 34). These constituencies were purposively selected because it is known from previous poverty mapping studies that they contain high concentrations of poor households (Sechaba Consultants 1991; 2000). They coincide with the six urban neighbourhoods of Lithoteng, Qoaling, Ha Seoli, Ha She-lile, Tsoapo-le-Bolila and Semphetenyane. The two constituencies are also sub-divided into 87 census units or enumeration areas. Four of the neighbourhoods – Seoli, Shelile, Tsoapo-le-Bolila and Semphetenyane – contain only 18 enumeration areas combined. For sampling purposes, they were therefore treated as if they constituted a single neighbourhood (hereafter SSTS) (Table 4). All three areas (Qoaling, Lithoteng and SSTS) have grown largely from the informal sub-division of agricultural land under the authority of local customary chiefs.[71] As a result, they consist of mixed income groups, with the poor and more wealthy located in very close proximity to each other. Because they have developed on the basis of private subdivisions, there is no discernible order in terms of streets, which made it impossible to draw a sample based on street networks and house numbers.

To ensure that the sample of 800 households was not spread too thinly across the constituencies, a decision was taken to sample only half of the 87 enumeration areas (Table 4). This meant that the 800 households were drawn from 43.5 enumeration areas. The distribution of the 800 households between the three neighbourhoods was determined through weighting/indexing. As a result, 344 (or 43% of the households) of the 800 households were drawn from Qoaling, 296 (37%) from Lithoteng and 20% (160) from SSTS (Table 4).

Neighbourhood	EAs	50% EAs sample size	% weight/ index	Sample size per area	Households per EA
Qoaling	37	18.5	43	344	18.6
Lithoteng	32	16	37	296	18.5
SSTS	18	9	20	160	17.7
Total	87	43.5	100	800	58.4

TABLE 4: Sampled Neighourhoods and Enumeration Areas

A complete list of enumeration area numbers for each of the three neigh-bourhoods was compiled from a digitized enumeration area map of Maseru city and a 50% (or k=2) systematic sample was drawn from the list.

Using aerial photomaps and enlarged printouts of the selected enumeration areas, the houses selected for interview were physically marked for each area. Pre-marking houses ensured that the sample was distributed evenly over each selected enumeration area. Given that the focus of the survey was the urban poor, an effort was made during the marking process to avoid structures that exhibited no obvious poverty attribute. However, some leeway was provided to research assistants to use their judgement to make appropriate substitutions where appropriate. The study areas also contain significant rental accommodation in rows of rooms or *maline* with each room usually occupied by an individual household. In such cases, research assistants were instructed to select the first door next to the entrance gate.

Another important aspect of the data collection strategy was the process of negotiating entry into the study areas. The first task was to consult the city councillors of the three study areas and explain the objectives of the study. The councillors in turn organized local community meetings (*lip-itso*) in their respective constituencies to inform residents of the impending study. These community meetings were augmented by three days of broadcasts over the national radio, in which the aims and owners of the research were announced, including the identities of the research assistants and who could be contacted for questions. This strategy was useful as the assistants found that in most households their visit was anticipated.

The survey instrument used was the standard AFSUN urban food security baseline survey developed collaboratively by the project partners. The survey collects basic demographic information on the household and its members, housing type, livelihoods, income-generating activity, food sources and levels of household food insecurity. AFSUN uses four international cross-cultural scales developed by the Food and Nutrition Technical Assistance Project (FANTA) to assess levels of food insecurity:

- Household Food Insecurity Access Scale (HFIAS): The HFIAS measures the degree of food insecurity during the month prior to the survey.[72] An HFIAS score is calculated for each household based on answers to nine "frequency-of-occurrence" questions. The minimum score is 0 and the maximum is 27. The higher the score, the more food insecurity the household experienced. The individual questions also provide insights into the nature of food insecurity experienced.

- Household Food Insecurity Access Prevalence Indicator (HFIAP): The HFIAP indicator uses the responses to the HFIAS questions to group households into four levels of household food insecurity: food secure, mildly food insecure, moderately food insecure and severely food insecure.[73]

- Household Dietary Diversity Scale (HDDS): Dietary diversity refers to how many food groups are consumed within the household in the previous 24 hours.[74] The maximum number, based on the FAO classification of food groups for Africa, is 12. An increase in the average number of different food groups consumed provides a quantifiable measure of improved household food access.

- Months of Adequate Household Food Provisioning Indicator (MAHFP): The MAHFP indicator captures changes in the household's ability to ensure that food is available above a minimum level the year round.[75] Households are asked to identify in which months (during the past 12) they did not have access to sufficient food to meet their household needs.

7. HOUSEHOLD PROFILE

Unlike many other Southern African cities, Maseru does not have large areas of informal settlement and shack dwellings. Most people (including those in the poorer parts of the city) live in basic housing made of brick and tin roofing on clearly demarcated plots. In the peri-urban areas, traditional rondavels (or *rontabole*) are more common as Maseru's urban sprawl has incorporated neighbouring rural villages. Of the 800 households surveyed, 61% lived in houses and 9% in traditional housing. Less than 0.5% were in informal shacks.

Most of the surveyed households in Maseru (80%) had between 1 and 5 members with an average household size of 4 members. Only Johannesburg and Gaborone in the 11-city AFSUN survey had such a high proportion of small households. Four main types of households can be identified, based on the sex and primary relationship of the household head: (a) female-centred households (headed by a single or formerly married woman without a male spouse or partner) (38% of households); (b) male-centred households (headed by a single or formerly married male without a female spouse or partner) (10% of households); (c) nuclear households of immediate blood relatives (usually male-headed with a female spouse or partner) (35% of households) and (d) extended households of immediate and distant relatives and non-relatives (again usually male-headed with a female spouse or partner) (17% of households). The distribution of Maseru households between these types is similar to Manzini in Swaziland and also to the regional average (Table 5).

TABLE 5: Type of Household by City											
	Wind-hoek	Gabo-rone	Ma-seru	Man-zini	Ma-puto	Blan-tyre	Lusaka	Harare	Cape Town	Msun-duzi	Johan-nes-burg	Total regional
Female-centred	33	47	38	38	27	19	20	23	42	53	33	34
Male-centred	21	23	10	17	8	6	3	7	11	12	16	12
Nuclear	23	20	35	32	21	41	48	37	34	22	36	32
Extended	24	8	17	12	45	34	28	33	14	13	15	22
Total	100	100	100	100	100	100	100	100	100	100	100	100
N	448	399	802	500	397	432	400	462	1,060	556	996	6,452

Household heads made up 25% of the individuals in sampled households and 13% were spouses or partners of the head. Some 39% were children and 12% grandchildren (Table 6). This indicates that the urban population of the poorer areas of Maseru is relatively youthful. As Figure 14 shows, 31% of the household members were under the age of 15 and another 24% were under the age of 25. Only 13% were over the age of 50. In total, 43% of the sample were married (predominantly in nuclear and extended households) and 38% were unmarried. The proportion of parents and grandparents of the head was extremely low (less than 1% combined), confirming that the elderly tend to reside in rural villages. Levels of formal education were generally low with only 8.6% of the sample having completed high school (and about 0.3% university). Over half (56%) of the household members were female and 44% male, a reflection of the in-migration of women to work in the textile factories over the last two decades.

TABLE 6: Demographic Characteristics of Household Members		No.	%
	Head	802	24.7
	Spouse/partner	419	12.9
	Son/daughter	1,254	38.6
	Adopted/foster child/orphan	42	1.3
	Father/mother	20	0.6
Relationship to household head	Brother/sister	159	4.9
	Grandchild	389	12.0
	Grandparent	7	0.2
	Son/daughter-in-law	32	1.0
	Other relative	103	3.2
	Non-relative	21	0.6
	Total	3,248	100.0

Sex	Male	1,424	44.0
	Female	1,811	56.0
	Total	3,235	100.0
Marital status (>=15 years)	Unmarried	871	38.7
	Married	973	43.2
	Living together	23	1.0
	Divorced	9	0.4
	Separated	112	5.0
	Abandoned	16	0.7
	Widowed	249	11.1
	Total	2,253	100.0
Highest level of education (>15 years)	No formal schooling	257	1.9
	Some primary school	1,122	38.9
	Primary school completed	515	17.9
	Some high school	741	25.7
	High school completed	177	6.1
	Post-secondary qualification	51	1.8
	Some university	11	0.4
	University completed	10	0.3
	Post-graduate	1	0.0
	Total	2,885	100.0

FIGURE 14: Age Distribution of Household Members

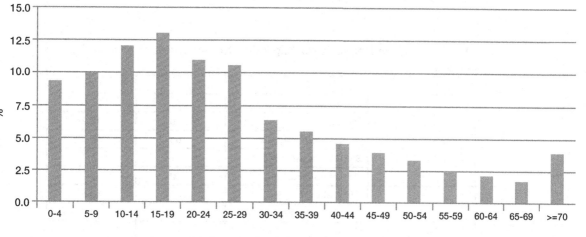

Half of the household members were born in Maseru, while 48% were born in a rural area and later moved to Maseru (Table 7). Only Gaborone and Windhoek of the 11 cities surveyed by AFSUN had a larger migrant population and a lower proportion of people born in the city of residence. Given the importance attached in the migration literature to economic and environmental factors as drivers of internal migration, it is noteworthy that social factors featured most prominently as the main motivation for moving to Maseru (Table 8). The prospect of informal employment rated more highly than formal sector employment, suggesting that migrants to the city are well aware of how difficult it is to access the formal labour market. Despite recurrent drought in Lesotho, which regularly leaves many in the rural areas in dire straits and in need of food aid, environmental factors and food insecurity were not given as major reasons for migration to Maseru. Only 1.5% cited food insecurity and hunger as the reason for migration and 0.2% that drought had precipitated the move.

TABLE 7: Place of Birth of Household Members in Surveyed Cities		
	Rural area %	Urban area %
Gaborone	68.6	28.4
Windhoek	51.2	48.0
Maseru	48.2	50.7
Cape Town	46.5	53.1
Msunduzi	45.6	53.7
Manzini	38.1	59.8
Johannesburg	31.0	64.7
Blantyre	26.2	72.5
Harare	25.5	72.9
Lusaka	23.0	76.4
Maputo	20.7	78.8

TABLE 8: Main Reasons for Migration to Maseru by Household Heads			
		No.	%
Social reasons	Moved with family	538	37.0
	Marriage	279	19.2
	Attractions of city life	88	6.0
	Sent to live with family	69	4.7
	Education/schooling	60	4.1
Livelihood/ economic reasons	Informal sector job	288	19.8
	Formal sector job	271	18.6
	Housing	121	8.3
	Overall living conditions	118	8.2
	Food/hunger	22	1.5
	Land for livestock/grazing	8	0.5
	Land for crop production	7	0.5
Environmental reasons	Drought	3	0.2
	Availability of water	2	0.1
Note: More than one answer permitted			

8. EMPLOYMENT, INCOMES AND HOUSEHOLD POVERTY

8.1 Employment, Migration and Unemployment

The official unemployment rate in Lesotho (defined as those without employment and looking for work) stood at 27% in 2008, having peaked at nearly 40% in 2003 (Figure 15). Domestic employment opportunities were relatively constrained until the early 1990s when the country experienced a large influx of manufacturing capital from Asia.[76] A sizable "sweatshop" garment industry grew in several urban centres with the majority of new factories in Maseru. The impetus behind the industry was Lesotho's status as a duty-free garment exporter to the US under that country's Africa Growth and Opportunities Act.[77] At its peak in 2006, there were nearly 50 foreign-owned factories employing close to 50,000 Basotho women. The largest producer was the Nien Hsing Group with three factories employing 7,500 people and producing 70,000 pairs of jeans a day for the US market.[78] Unemployment in Lesotho declined with the growth of the textile industry after 2000 but has remained stubbornly high at 25-30% in recent years.

FIGURE 15: Unemployment Rate in Lesotho, 1991-2012

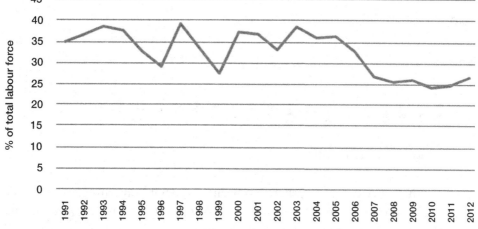

Source: World Bank (2014)

The low wages associated with garment factory employment forces many young women to live in high density and substandard rented accommodation in peri-urban areas.[79] For instance, in Ha Tsolo and Ha Tikoe, which are popular with people employed in the garment factories, over 70% of households are tenants. Although there are more women than men in Lesotho's urban areas, there is an increase in the movement of young men to Maseru in search of local income-earning opportunities, especially in the informal economy. This is largely because the South African demand for unskilled male labour from Lesotho has declined.

A considerable number of Lesotho citizens live and work in South Africa's major cities. For decades, this migration corridor was dominated by young men working in the South African gold mines. After 1990, as the industry went into decline, the number of Basotho migrant mineworkers in South Africa declined considerably from 121,000 in 1990 to only 43,000 in 2009 (a decline of 65%) (Figure 16).[80] The actual numbers are undoubtedly higher since many ex-miners participate in a dangerous but thriving illegal gold mining industry in South Africa.

FIGURE 16: Migrant Miners from Lesotho in South Africa, 1986-2009

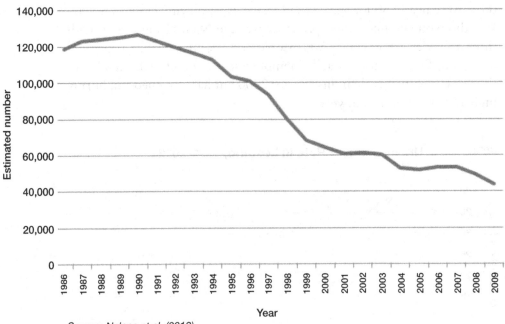

Source: Nalane et al. (2012)

In the last two decades, there has been considerable age and gender diversification in the employment and activity profile of Basotho migrants in South African cities. The South African domestic work sector is now a major employer of female Basotho migrants, many of whom are undocumented.[81] In 2011, there were 135,000 migrants from Lesotho in South Africa (of whom 36% were women) (Table 9). The vast majority were short-term migrants (with 85% having been away for less than a year and only 3% for more than 3 years). The majority of both male and female migrants were of working age and in wage employment or seeking work in South Africa (Table 10). One of the major benefits of migration to South Africa is the flow of remittances to Lesotho. Although the number of migrant mineworkers has been in decline since the early 1990s, this has been compensated for by increases in other forms of migration.

TABLE 9: Migrants from Lesotho in South Africa by Age and Sex, 2011			
Age group	Male	Female	Total
0-4	1,331	1,853	3,184
5-9	864	1,175	2,040
10-14	1,190	1,163	2,353
15-19	2,938	2,769	5,707
20-24	11,060	6,963	18,023
25-29	15,876	8,753	24,628
30-34	14,023	6,691	20,714
35-39	10,961	4,863	15,824
40-44	8,496	3,460	11,956
45-49	7,640	3,629	11,269
50-54	6,245	3,119	9,364
55-59	3,884	1,984	5,868
60-64	1,383	701	2,084
65-69	680	618	1,298
70-74	104	231	335
75-79	80	226	306
80-84	29	37	67
85+	47	41	87
Do not know	70	108	178
Total	86,900	48,384	135,285
Source: LDS (2012)			

TABLE 10: Occupations of Lesotho Migrants in South Africa, 2011		
	No.	%
Wage employment	87,390	68.0
Casual work	9,789	7.6
Accompanying spouse	9,031	7.0
Student	9,013	7.0
Looking for work	7,028	5.4
Informal worker	4,982	3.9
Other	2,137	1.7
Total	129,369	100.0
Source: LDS (2012)		

Just over a quarter (28%) of the adult population in the surveyed Maseru households were employed full-time (either in Maseru itself or South Africa) and a fifth (21%) were in part-time or casual employment. As many as half of the adults were unemployed (including the 27% who were looking for work) (Table 11). Around 10% of employed household members were away working in South Africa. Maseru is home to some of Lesotho's 40,000 migrant miners working in South Africa (unlike in the past when virtually all miners were from rural households). Around 6% of household members with jobs were working on the mines in South Africa. Apart from the miners, the other major sources of employment in South Africa (especially for women) are domestic work and farm work. However, the survey turned up only a few farm workers so it is likely that many of the other migrants were domestic workers.

TABLE 11: Employment Status of Adult Household Members in Maseru		
	No.	%
Working full-time	538	27.6
Working part-time/casual	411	21.1
Working-status unknown	15	0.8
Not working – looking for work	527	27.0
Not working – not looking for work	454	23.3
Not working – status unknown	4	0.2
Total	1,949	100.0

Only a very small proportion of those with jobs were employed in more skilled occupations such as office work, health work and teaching (all less than 2%) (Table 12). The vast majority of households with a wage income had members who were employed in unskilled, low wage jobs or were working in the informal economy. As many as one-third of household members worked as unskilled manual labourers. Just under 10% worked in the informal economy as producers, vendors and traders and around 9% ran their own businesses. Other low-skilled jobs included domestic work (7%) and service work (3%).

One occupation that does not appear in official statistics and falls under the "other" category in the AFSUN survey is commercial sex work. Another study interviewed over 100 female commercial sex workers (CSWs) and found that over half were migrants to Maseru, with the youngest aged 13 and the oldest slightly over 40 years. The average age was 21. All CSWs were functionally literate, having completed seven years of primary education. Nearly 70% had some secondary education and a few had post-secondary or tertiary training, but all had dropped out due to lack of money.[82] Most CSWs worked full-time, while others did sex work to supplement their factory wages. Most full-time CSWs had no other work experience. The reasons given for engaging in commercial sex were poverty (the need to earn money) and lack of jobs. Average weekly income was estimated at LSL400, which was nearly equivalent to the monthly wage of a mechanist in a textile factory.[83] Local and central government are extremely intolerant of CSWs and police have been known to arrest CSWs on Maseru streets under the provisions of the colonial Vagrancy Act of 1879, as there is no law that expressly bars commercial sex work.[84]

TABLE 12: Main Occupation of Employed Household Members			
		No.	%
Skilled	Skilled manual worker	70	7.5
	Teacher	15	1.6
	Office worker	11	1.2
	Civil servant	10	1.1
	Professional worker	9	1.0
	Supervisor	8	0.8
	Health worker	3	0.3
	Employer/manager	1	0.1
Semi-skilled	Mine worker	58	6.1
	Service worker	26	2.7
	Truck driver	18	1.9
	Police/military	15	1.6
	Farmer	6	0.6
Low skilled	Manual worker	306	32.3
	Domestic worker	71	7.5
	Agricultural worker	10	1.1
Self-employed	Business owner	88	9.3
Informal employment	Informal economy	89	9.4
Other		103	10.9
Total		947	100.0

8.2 Household Incomes and Poverty

The mean household income during the month prior to the survey was LSL700. This means that half the households had an income of less than USD87 or about USD2.90 per day. Based on a mean household size of 5, that works out to be less than USD0.60 per person per day. Wage employment proved to be the major source of household income with 39% of households receiving income from formal work and 39% from casual work (Table 13). The informal economy provided income for only 14% of households. The other two relatively important income sources were remittances from South Africa (received by 15% of households) and social grants (13% of households). While wage work easily generated the highest mean monthly income, remittances were more important than casual work, informal activity or social grants. Most households (90%) had more than one income-generating strategy and some (42%) had as many as four or more.

TABLE 13: Sources of Household Income

	No. of house-holds	% of house-holds	Mean monthly amount (LSL)	Minimum (LSL)	Maxi-mum (LSL)
Wage work	314	39.1	1,330	70	8,500
Casual work	310	38.6	451	20	4,800
Remittances	123	15.3	754	10	6,000
Informal business	112	14.0	485	50	5,000
Social grants	107	13.3	288	100	3,000
Rent	51	4.3	400	40	1,970
Gifts	21	1.8	125	10	1,600
Sale of rural farm products	17	1.4	597	25	4,000
Sale of urban farm products	17	1.4	771	20	4,000
Formal business	14	1.2	983	30	4,000
Note: More than one answer permitted					

The survey did not collect data on income predictability but it can be assumed that households with a regular wage earner are likely to experience much lower income fluctuation than those whose primary source of income is casual work or the informal economy or who have several income-generating strategies. A separate survey in July 2008 asked urban households in Lesotho whether their income had changed in the previous six months.[85] In the case of Maseru, 24% said that it had increased, 32% said that it had remained the same and 44% said that it had decreased.[86] Households dependent on wage employment were least likely to have experienced a decline in income over this period. What this suggests is that it was not just rising food prices that impacted on many poor urban households in 2007–2008 but declining and unpredictable income.

One of the most common food-related indicators of poverty is how much of its income a household spends on food. The draws on household income are many; the vast majority of households incur monthly expenditures on food (purchased by 94% of households), fuel (by 88%) and utilities such as water and electricity (by 87%) (Table 14). Half incurred costs for transportation and 45% for education (mainly school fees and uniforms). Around a third paid for insurance and housing. A quarter had medical expenses and 19% sent money to relatives in rural areas. Very few (8%) were able to save; indeed, more households spent money on funerals and debt repayment than on savings. On the Lived Poverty Index, a robust measure of self-assessed poverty, only Manzini, Harare and Lusaka had worse scores than Maseru (Figure 17).

TABLE 14: Household Expenditure Categories					
	No. of house-holds	% of house-holds	Mean (LSL)	Minimum (LSL)	Maximum (LSL)
Food and groceries	669	94.0	322	5	2,000
Fuel	625	88.0	155	10	1,500
Utilities	619	87.0	77	5	2,075
Transportation	345	50.0	160	7	868
Education	320	45.0	104	2	750
Insurance	263	37.0	38	0	400
Housing	236	33.0	109	25	500
Medical expenses	183	26.0	27	0	583
Remittances	132	19.0	63	0	667
Debt service/repayment	88	11.0	147	2	1,752
Funeral costs	69	10.0	207	3	833
Savings	60	8.0	355	20	3,000
Goods purchased to sell	40	5.5	255	0	2,000
Home-based care	37	5.0	48	0	417

FIGURE 17: Comparative Lived Poverty Index Scores

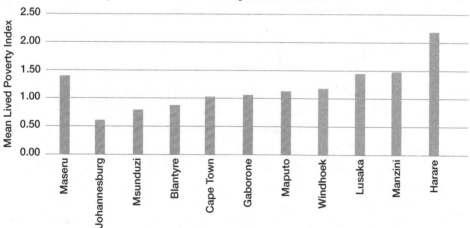

9. HOUSEHOLD SOURCES OF FOOD

Poor households in Maseru obtain their food from a variety of sources and with varying frequency (Table 15). Around half of the households (47%) said they obtain some of their food from urban agriculture, but only 21% do so on a regular basis (at least once a week). A similar proportion of households (49%) source food from the informal economy, at least a third on a regular basis and 11% daily. As many as 84% of the households shop at supermarkets. The majority (62%) do so monthly and 21% at least once a week. Easily the most important source of food on a daily and weekly basis are small retail outlets and fast-food nodes. Other food-access strategies include the bartering of household goods for food; laundry, babysitting, brewing and sale of wild vegetables in exchange for cash or food; borrowing or buying food on credit; and attending funerals and feasts for free food.[87]

TABLE 15: Household Food Sources by Frequency of Use						
	Never %	At least five days a week %	At least once a week %	At least once a month %	At least once in six months %	Less than once a year %
Small shop/ restaurant/take away	11	27	50	12	1	<1
Supermarkets	16	4	17	62	1	0
Informal market/street food	51	11	23	11	2	2
Urban agriculture	53	8	13	9	13	3
Borrow food from others	59	4	12	19	4	1
Food provided by other households	71	2	10	11	4	2
Shared meal with other households	80	2	8	7	1	2
Food remittances	86	<1	1	5	5	2
Food aid	97	<1	<1	2	1	<1
Note: More than one answer permitted						

9.1 Urban Agriculture

The traditional land use pattern in rural Lesotho involved locating villages on the slopes of sandstone hills and devoting the productive plains around these hills to crop farming and the less productive areas to grazing. Until recent decades, this was the prevailing settlement structure in the villages that today fall within the urban boundary of Maseru. As Maseru expanded, arable land declined from 31% of the total land within the urban boundary in 1989 to only 7% in 2000.[88] Recent studies have confirmed that urban expansion and in-filling has led to wholesale conversion of agricultural land to residential development.[89] Some alluvial plains along the Caledon and Phuthiatsana rivers are still devoted to crop farming and to government-supported irrigated commercial vegetable farming. In the main, however, open field agriculture within the city boundary has largely been substituted with small-scale household garden plots. In 2000, it was estimated that over 26,000 or 28% of households in Maseru were engaged in some form of agriculture and that, of those, 1,500 or 6% considered urban agriculture as their main source of income.[90] Two-thirds of household members in urban agriculture households contributed labour to this activity. In addition, over 1,000 labourers were hired for planting and over 8,000 for weeding in the city.

The most common urban household agricultural activities within Maseru include home gardens, particularly by low and middle-income households; small-scale backyard commercial poultry and egg production and piggeries; large-scale commercial poultry farming by a small number of producers; milk production by members of the Lesotho Dairy Association; and subsistence livestock and crop farming, an activity that is usually associated with households that continue to lead rural lifestyles or with those in traditional villages within the city boundary. Commercial poultry and eggs and milk are often sold at the farm-gate although some farmers supply a few commercial outlets. However, only 2% of households surveyed said that they obtained any income from the sale of urban agricultural products.

In Maseru, 31% of the surveyed households had gardens (Table 16), a higher proportion than in any other city surveyed by AFSUN. Only 8% had fields and 9% had livestock. However, only 20% said that they regularly (at least once a week) ate home-grown produce. Nearly a third of households said they were partly or totally dependent on garden crops, compared with less than 10% who said they depended on field crops, tree crops or livestock. The survey also found that 47% of households grew some of the food they consumed.

TABLE 16: Household Dependence on Urban Agriculture			
Type	Dependence level	No. of households	% of households
Field crops	Totally dependent	30	4
	Partly dependent	31	4
	Slightly dependent	42	5
	Not at all	696	87
Garden crops	Totally dependent	76	10
	Partly dependent	170	21
	Slightly dependent	239	30
	Not at all	313	39
Tree crops	Totally dependent	8	1
	Partly dependent	37	5
	Slightly	117	15
	Not at all	636	79
Livestock	Totally dependent	37	5
	Partly dependent	37	5
	Slightly	54	7
	Not at all	671	84

A recurrent question in the literature on urban agriculture is whether the poorest and most food insecure households participate more than better-off households.[91] In the case of Maseru, the answer is very clear. Even in generally poor neighbourhoods, the poorest are less likely to engage in urban agriculture (Table 17). Only 33% of households in the lowest income tercile had used urban agriculture as a food source in the previous year compared to 51% of households in the upper income tercile. There was a similar relationship with the Lived Poverty Index. As the LPI increases (indicating more poverty), so the proportion of households involved in urban agriculture decreases.

TABLE 17: Household Urban Agriculture Utilization as Food Source Over the Previous Year				
Variable	Category	Yes (%)	No (%)	N
Household income	Low income	33	67	231
	Middle income	46	54	224
	High income	51	49	245
Lived Poverty Index	0-1	47	53	280
	1-2	43	57	347
	2-3	35	65	124
	3-4	21	79	14

There is some evidence that the area under urban agriculture in Maseru may have declined since the AFSUN survey was implemented. The Bureau of Statistics has published an annual urban agriculture report since 2008/9 and although the time series figures differ between reports there appears to have been a rather dramatic decline in the area planted to vegetables by households. According to the reports, the area covered by urban vegetable plots in Maseru District declined from 5.8 million square metres in 2008/9 to 2.8 million in 2010/11 to 370,000 in 2011/12.[92] Cabbage, spinach and rape were the most important vegetables grown. In addition, the number of cattle owned by urban households in Maseru District decreased from 62,638 in 2008/9 to 34,009 in 2011/12.[93] That said, in 2009/10, there appeared to be a spike in urban agriculture engagement. In 2009 and 2010, 19,686,543 square meters of land in Maseru was planted with vegetables and 98,111 cattle were owned by households in Maseru.[94] It seems that, while engagement in urban agriculture may have decreased, the practice is still implemented during times of food insecurity (as exemplified by the repercussions of the 2008 food price crisis). Among Maseru households that own cattle, 23.2% use the cattle for milk, 35.2% use the cattle for milk and meat, while 41.6% use the cattle for milk and draught.

9.2 Informal Food Sources

The majority of informal sector enterprises are one-person operations, with few partnerships or co-ownership. Informal sector activities are varied, but in the main consist of small-scale manufacturing, street vending and other types of trade activities, construction, services and transport. There are six categories of operation:[95]

- Traders of non-food manufactured and artisan goods, such as electrical and mobile phone accessories, clothing (often second-hand) and leather items (wallets, belts, shoes, jackets), jewellery, curios and handicrafts;

- Traders of non-food services, including shoe, watch and bicycle repairs, car washing and car parking attendants;

- Vendors of fruits and vegetables;

- Vendors of prepared meals;

- Combination traders of food and non-food services;

- Other traders, including vendors of traditional herbs and medicines, sweets and other processed treats, skin and hair care products, vegetable seeds, as well as distributors of newspapers, cigarettes, mobile phone airtime and so forth.

While women have traditionally dominated street activities, there has been a increase in the number of young men joining this sector, especially in new enterprises. Most of the vendors in one study were migrants from other parts of country who had come to Maseru looking for formal sector work.[96] Young men who cannot find factory or similar work turn to informal trading as their primary source of livelihood. Relations between street vendors and the city authorities have been characterized by harassment by the national police and city council officials, with damaging effects on the livelihoods of street vendors.[97]

Despite the size of the informal sector in Lesotho, and its role in the urban food supply system, Maseru households were far less reliant on the informal food economy than poor households in many other cities surveyed by AFSUN. Only Gaborone, Manzini and Msunduzi households were less dependent on informal food sources (Table 18). In the year prior to the survey, 49% of Maseru households had accessed food from informal sources: 11% on a daily basis and 23% at least once a week. In most other cities, over two-thirds of poor households were regular patrons of informal vendors (over 90% in cities such as Lusaka, Maputo, Harare and Blantyre).

TABLE 18: Use of Informal Food Sources by City	
	Informal economy (% of households)
Lusaka	99
Maputo	98
Harare	97
Blantyre	96
Johannesburg	84
Windhoek	75
Cape Town	66
Maseru	49
Manzini	46
Msunduzi	42
Gaborone	29

9.3 Formal Retail

As the Lesotho population has become more urbanized and exposed to non-traditional diets, so its food preferences and food tastes have changed. The country imports most of the foods that increasingly characterize the Basotho urban diet. The food import trade is dominated by South African wholesalers and retailers and, increasingly, supermarket chains. In the last decade all major South African supermarket chains have opened outlets in Maseru's CBD. Some, such as Pick n Pay, Woolworths, Shoprite and Fruit & Veg City, are located in CBD West, close to middle and high-income residential areas. Shoprite has a branch in CBD East, close to lower-income areas of the city and surrounded by informal traders and hawkers (see cover photo). The supermarkets source the vast majority of their fresh and processed food from South Africa and via South African distribution centres. They are, therefore, firmly integrated into South African supply chains and responsible for a significant proportion of food imports from South Africa. Opportunities for local suppliers, especially in Maseru itself, are extremely limited (see Box 2).

As many as 84% of the surveyed households regularly source food from supermarkets, one of the highest proportions in the region. Given the relatively small size of Maseru, no residential area is completely inaccessible to supermarket penetration. At the same time, there is a distinct pattern of supermarket patronage with only 21% shopping there at least once a week and 62% doing so on a monthly basis. This suggests that poor urban households prefer to patronize supermarkets to buy cereal staples (such as maize meal) in bulk once a month (mostly on or around payday). The expansion of South African supermarkets has exercised considerable competitive pressure on much smaller locally-owned groceries and supermarket outlets. However, these outlets are scattered around the city and are close to the neighbourhoods surveyed by AFSUN.

BOX 2: Supplying Supermarkets

An estimated 99 percent of supermarket goods are imported from South African agribusinesses through border posts. That leaves little room for 73-year-old Tseliso Lebentlele, who farms a sliver of land in Maseru, the capital city next to the border. He pulled on his wool hat against the chill, then walked down the narrow rows. Like most small farmers, he carries all the financial risks himself, and he's been wiped out time and again. His crops have been stolen by thieves and trampled by cattle. Last year, he managed to lease a field out of town and was about to harvest green beans and pumpkins. "And floods just wiped me out completely," Lebentlele said. "I had to start from scratch." But he keeps trying. "People in farming have sawdust in our heads," he said. "We carry on regardless." The farmers union in Lesotho is just getting started, and the government is weak, so there are few advocates for farmers like Lebentlele. He bought a few pigs, but the supermarkets told him that they don't trust the hygiene standards of local butchers. "These supermarkets will not touch them," he said. "Because – look, if anything, let's say, were to go wrong, then they would be liable." So he's growing a few rows of cabbage and spinach in a borrowed greenhouse. They're beautiful. But alone, he just can't produce at the scale that the supermarkets want. "I'm scared of going to these companies and saying to them, 'Look, I can supply you with this and this,' " Lebentlele said. "Because I am a small man. If you cannot supply on a continuous basis, it is very, very difficult to hold markets."

Source: PBS Newshour, 26 September 2012

Many small retail outlets call themselves supermarkets but are in fact small-scale grocers, corner stores and butcheries. The exact number is unknown, although one survey did find 21 butcheries in the Maseru District in 2007.[98] Most of these suppliers are locally owned although there is a significant, and controversial, Chinese presence.[99] In 2010, 313 out of 2,518 registered wholesale and retail businesses in Lesotho were owned by Chinese immigrants, mainly from Fujian Province in China.[100] As one study of the expansion of Chinese traders throughout Lesotho notes:

> Regardless of their legal status, Chinese shops play different roles, depending on their actual location. In larger towns, they provide a welcome alternative to the sometimes pricey durable consumer

goods sold in South African supermarkets, which often source the same low-quality products from China, but sell them at a much higher price. Although food products sold in Chinese shops some-times have a negative image because of an allegedly widespread practice of "re-labelling" expired goods, the Chinese shops were bustling with customers.[101]

What is clear from the AFSUN survey is that smaller retail outlets, both Chinese and Basotho-owned, play a major role in the urban food system of Maseru, somewhat akin to that of the informal food economy in other Southern African cities. Only 11% of the surveyed households said that they never shop for food at these outlets. Of the remaining 89%, 27% source their food there on a daily basis and 50% at least once a week. This heavy reliance on small retail outlets is unique to Maseru when com-pared with the other cities surveyed. Since many of the South African supermarkets are relatively new arrivals, it remains to be seen whether their presence is changing shopping habits or whether the small food retail sector is displaying resilience. This is an area requiring further research although the spread of Chinese small shops throughout Lesotho has been attributed, at least in part, to competitive pressure in the urban centres.[102]

9.4 Social Protection

A recent overview of formal social protection in Lesotho optimistically concludes that the country "has already achieved an impressive record in incrementally building a basic assistance system and a social protection floor. It has made substantial progress along the road to developing social protection initiatives to provide minimum levels of protection to everyone … and introducing social assistance measures targeting the indigent and vulnerable."[103] These programmes include a universal old-age pension (OAP) for those over 70, a child-grant programme, free primary health care and subsidized health services at public facilities, indigent support, orphans and vulnerable children support, free primary education and food security measures. Food security measures include government-funded subsidized inputs to farmers, donor-driven food aid in the form of food-for-work, and food and cash transfer programmes during times of acute stress (most notably during and after the 2007 drought). However, these programmes are generally "reactive, short-lived, selective and pro-tective."[104] Since they also tend to target rural populations, it is perhaps unsurprising that 97% of households in the Maseru survey reported never being recipients of food aid.

More relevant in the urban context are what are generally referred to as "informal social protection" mechanisms. Turner's comparative analysis of the same rural village in Lesotho in 1976 and 2004 found that some inter-household, intra-village livelihood sharing practices (particularly farming-related) had declined but that others persisted.[105] Amongst the residents in 2004, there was a sense that mutuality and sharing had declined in importance over the years:

> The majority view … is that the community spirit is in decline, and that people help each other less than they did previously. Support from parents, children or other relatives is still often cited as a significant livelihood strategy, but (doubtless with a tinge of nostalgia) most people believe that life is becoming more individualistic. Only in death, they say, does the community still unite to help the bereaved household. Overall, the effectiveness of the community as provider of social protection is weaker than it was. However, this view is not unanimous, and some say that the Sesotho spirit of helping each other is still strong.[106]

Whether the "Sesotho spirit" is waning or is still strong in the countryside, it appears from the AFSUN survey that it is not being reproduced in the more competitive and less cooperative urban environment where bonds of kinship and locality are weaker, at least in regard to hunger and food security. A total of 80% of surveyed households had never shared a meal with another household and 71% had never consumed food given to them by another household. Borrowing food was more common, but 59% of households had never obtained food in this way. Amongst those who did obtain food in these three ways, it was a fairly regular occurrence. This suggests that it is probably the poorest and most destitute households that rely on informal social protection for food. The vast majority simply have to fend for themselves. Given that the surveyed areas of Maseru do not only contain poor households, it seems that the poor do not benefit from the presence of better-off neighbours.

The final social protection question is whether residents of Maseru, many of whom are migrants to the city, benefit from their links with rural villages. Some cities surveyed by AFSUN, such as Windhoek, receive large informal food transfers from the rural areas.[107] In the case of Maseru households, only 23% had received food from relatives and friends in the rural areas in the year prior to the survey. Given the state of agriculture in Lesotho's countryside and the tendency of rural households to consume whatever they produce, this is perhaps not surprising. Indeed, more households (24%) had received food from relatives and friends living in other urban areas (especially in South Africa). Nearly two-thirds (63%) of the rural-urban transfers were cereals (maize and sorghum) and most of the rest (32%) were vegetables (Table 19). In contrast, urban-urban transfers were more varied: cereals (34%) and vegetables (28%) were still dominant but a number of Maseru households also received cooking oil, meat/poultry and sugar. Notably, neither form of transfer included much fruit or many eggs.

TABLE 19: Informal Food Transfers to Maseru		
	% of rural-urban transfers	% of urban-urban transfers
Cereals (foods made from grain)	62.7	34.2
Foods made from beans, peas, lentils, or nuts	25.0	8.5
Vegetables	7.0	19.5
Roots or tubers	2.0	3.9
Meat or poultry or offal	1.6	7.5
Fruits	0.4	2.8
Fresh or dried fish or shellfish	0.4	2.1
Cheese, yoghurt, milk or other milk products	0.4	3.9
Eggs	0.0	2.8
Foods made with oil, fat, or butter	0.4	9.5
Sugar or honey	0.0	5.4
N	244	389
Note: More than one answer permitted		

The survey also found an important difference in timing between rural-urban and urban-urban transfers (Table 20). The former tended to be infrequent. For example, only 17% of households benefitting from rural-urban food transfers of cereals did so more than once a month. Around half received transfers once a year, presumably at harvest time. In contrast, those benefitting from urban-urban transfers did so far more often, with 35% of cereal transfers occurring weekly and 47% at least once every two months. Only 10% of households received urban-urban cereal transfers on an annual basis.

TABLE 20: Frequency of Informal Food Transfers		
	Rural-urban transfers (% recipient households)	Urban-urban transfers (% recipient households)
At least once a week	2	35
At least once every two months	17	47
3-6 times per year	29	8
At least once per year	52	10
N	151	133

10. LEVELS OF FOOD INSECURITY IN MASERU

The AFSUN survey found that levels of food insecurity in Maseru were amongst the worst in the region, exceeded only by cities in countries in severe economic crisis (Zimbabwe and Swaziland). The Household Food Insecurity Access Scale (HFIAS) score for surveyed households, for example, was an extremely high 12.8, well above the regional average of 10.3 (Table 21). Of all the cities surveyed, only Harare and Manzini had higher scores. At the same time, there was wide variation in HFIAS scores with some households scoring 0 (complete food security) and some 27 (critical food insecurity). However, most of the households had very high scores: 50% of households had HFIAS scores higher than the mean and 20% had scores of 20 or more (Table 22).

TABLE 21: HFIAS Averages by City			
	Mean	Median	N
Manzini	14.9	14.7	489
Harare	14.7	16.0	454
Maseru	12.8	13.0	795
Lusaka	11.5	11.0	386
Msunduzi	11.3	11.0	548
Gaborone	10.8	11.0	391
Cape Town	10.7	11.0	1,026
Maputo	10.4	10.0	389
Windhoek	9.3	9.0	436
Blantyre	5.3	3.7	431
Johannesburg	4.7	1.5	976
Region	10.3	10	6,327

TABLE 22: HFIAS Scores for Maseru		
HFIAS score	% of households	Cumulative %
0	3.7	3.7
1	2.0	5.7
2	1.9	7.6
3	2.8	10.4
4	2.9	13.3
5	3.1	16.4
6	3.3	19.7
7	5.5	25.2
8	4.3	29.5
9	4.2	33.7

10	5.5	39.2
11	3.9	43.1
12	6.7	49.8
13	5.4	55.2
14	5.2	60.4
15	6.3	66.9
16	3.0	69.9
17	3.0	72.9
18	4.9	77.8
19	2.9	80.7
20	3.3	84.0
21	3.5	87.5
22	1.9	89.4
23	2.4	91.8
24	1.8	93.6
25	2.1	95.7
26	0.5	96.2
27	3.8	100.0
N = 795		

The severity of food insecurity in Maseru was confirmed by the HFIAP, which divides households into four food security categories. Just 5% of the households fell into the completely food secure category (Table 23). Only Harare and Lusaka had a lower percentage of completely food secure households. Twenty-five percent of Maseru households were moderately food insecure and 65% were severely food insecure. More cities had higher proportions of severely food insecure households however, including Cape Town and Manzini as well as Harare and Lusaka.

TABLE 23: HFIAP Categories by City

	Food secure %	Mildly food insecure %	Moderately food insecure %	Severely food insecure %
Harare	2	3	24	72
Lusaka	4	3	24	69
Maseru	5	6	25	65
Maputo	5	9	32	54
Manzini	6	3	13	79
Msunduzi	7	6	27	60
Gaborone	12	6	19	63
Cape Town	15	5	12	68
Windhoek	18	5	14	63
Blantyre	34	15	30	21
Johannesburg	44	14	15	27
Region	16	7	20	57

The limited diversity of the Maseru diet was evident in HDDS scores. Of all the cities surveyed by AFSUN, Maseru households had the lowest dietary diversity, consuming on average food from only 3.4 food groups over the previous 24 hours (Figure 18). Over 60% of the households had a score of 3 or less (Table 24). By contrast, only 23% of poor households across the region had scores of 3 or less. At the other end of the scale, only 16% of Maseru households had scores of 6 or more, compared with 51% across the region. The two dominant foods in the diet were cereals (largely maize and sorghum, consumed by almost all households) and some kind of vegetable (consumed by 70% of households). Only 21% of households had consumed meat or chicken and 8% of households had consumed fruit over the previous 24 hours. A recent study of nutritional knowledge and dietary behaviour among women in urban and rural Lesotho confirmed the extremely low dietary diversity in the Basotho diet with heavy daily reliance on maize porridge (pap) and relish (leafy vegetables) and only occasional consumption of meat and dairy products.[108] Many of the women interviewed for the study noted that the price of these foodstuffs had put them out of reach as part of the regular diet.

FIGURE 18: Household Dietary Diversity by City

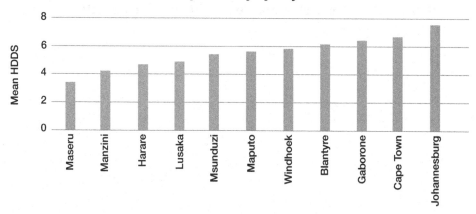

TABLE 24: Maseru and Regional Dietary Diversity Scores

HDDS	Maseru % of households	Maseru cumulative %	Region % of households	Region cumulative %
0	1	1	0	0
1	7	8	2	2
2	34	42	11	13
3	21	63	10	23
4	11	74	11	34
5	11	85	15	48
6	6	91	14	62
7	5	96	12	74

8	3	99	10	84
9	1	–	7	91
10	<1	–	4	95
11	<1	–	2	97
12	<1	100	3	100
N	768		6,327	

Given that Lesotho imports the vast majority of food that is consumed in the country, it is of interest to see if there is any monthly variation to the household experience of food insecurity in Maseru. The average MAHFP score was 7.76, i.e. the average number of months in which households had adequate food was between 7 and 8 months. The proportion of households that reported having an adequate supply of food over the previous year varied from a high of 73% in December 2007 to a low of 45% in June 2008, and remained around 50% for the rest of the year (Figure 19). Rather than any marked seasonality in food access (as was the case in many other cities), the Maseru data shows a consistent decline in the proportion of households with adequate food provisioning as 2008 progressed. This is one clear indicator of the impact of rising food prices.

FIGURE 19: Months of Adequate Household Food Provisioning

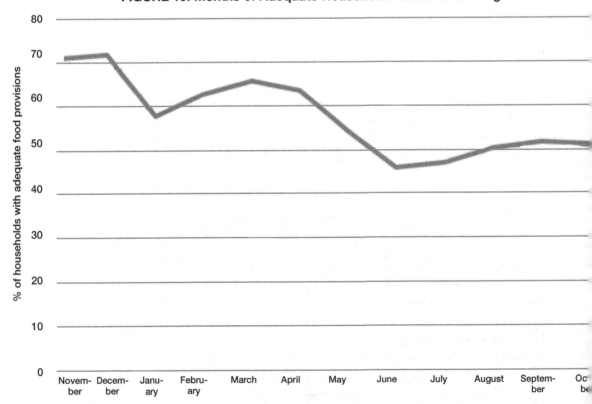

11. HOUSEHOLD VARIATIONS IN LEVELS OF FOOD INSECURITY

11.1 Demographic Variables, Income and Poverty

The previous section demonstrated that although the vast majority of Maseru's poor households are food insecure, there is some inter-household variability. This section focuses on the reasons for these variations by looking first at household structure and then at other inter-household differences. Cross-tabulation of household type by the four HFIAP food insecurity categories reveals some differences, though these are not statistically significant (Table 25). For example, there were slightly fewer food secure and slightly more severely food insecure female-centred households than male-centred households. However, in every household type between 60% and 70% of households were severely food insecure. When food secure and mildly food insecure households are combined into a single category, the difference between male-centred and female-centred households is stronger. Only 7% of female-centred households fall into the food secure and mildly food insecure categories, compared to 14% of male-centred households, 13% of extended households and 12% of nuclear households.

TABLE 25: Levels of Food Insecurity by Household Type				
	Food secure (%)	Mild food insecurity (%)	Moderate food insecurity (%)	Severe food insecurity (%)
Female-centred	3	4	27	67
Male-centred	8	6	20	66
Nuclear	5	7	27	61
Extended	7	6	22	66

As might be expected, there is a strong association between household income and food insecurity (Table 26). Thus, 82% of households in the lowest income tercile were severely food insecure compared with 46% of households in the upper income tercile. Likewise, less than 1% of households in the lowest income tercile were completely food secure compared to 9% in the upper income tercile. A similar pattern can be seen with the Lived Poverty Index. As the LPI score increases (increasing poverty), so does the proportion of severely food insecure households. While households with one livelihood strategy (usually wage employment) had the lowest levels of food insecurity, it does not follow that food security increased with an increasing number of strategies. The incidence of severe food insecurity was very similar whether a household had three or more strategies.

TABLE 26: Levels of Household Food Insecurity by Economic Indicators				
	Food secure (%)	Mild food insecurity (%)	Moderate food insecurity (%)	Severe food insecurity (%)
Income				
Poorest (<LSL420)	0	4	14	82
Less poor (LSL20-999)	3	3	30	64
Least poor (>LSL999)	8	10	36	46
Lived Poverty Index score				
0-1	12	12	42	34
1-2	1	3	20	76
2-3	0	0	5	95
3-4	0	0	0	100
No. of livelihood strategies				
1	6	12	30	52
2	4	5	32	59
3	5	4	23	68
4	2	9	20	69
5+	7	3	24	66

A finer-grained analysis on inter-household variation is possible by cross-tabulating a number of variables with the means scores for each of the three quantitative food security measures (the HFIAS, HDDS and MAHFP) (Table 27). First, there is a clear relationship between household size and food insecurity on two of the indicators: the HFIAS and the MAHFP. As household size increased, so did food insecurity as measured by the HFIAS (from 12.5 amongst households with 1-5 members to 14.5 for those with more than 10 members). Similarly, the MAHFP consistently fell with increasing household size (indicating a greater number of months with inadequate food provisioning as size increases). The slight anomaly was with the HDDS: households with 1-5 members had the highest score (at 3.5) while both categories of larger household had the same score (3.0). However, as noted above, the HDDS for all three groups is extremely low and amongst the lowest in the region.

TABLE 27: Mean Household Food Security Scores by Household Characteristics			
Household size	HFIAS	HDDS	MAHFP
1-5	12.5	3.5	8.0
6-10	14.2	3.0	6.9
>10	14.5	3.0	7.7
Household type			
Female-centred	14.1	3.5	7.3
Male-centred	12.4	3.2	7.8
Nuclear	11.9	3.5	8.2
Extended	12.0	3.6	7.9
Sex of head			
Female	14.1	3.5	7.4
Male	11.9	3.4	8.0
Income tercile			
Lowest(<LSL420)	16.4	2.8	6.3
Middle (LSL420-999)	13.1	3.2	8.0
Highest (>LSL999)	9.4	4.4	9.1
LPI score			
0.00-1.00	7.6	6.24	9.6
1.01-2.00	14.5	5.32	7.4
2.01-3.00	18.3	4.50	5.4
3.01-4.00	25.3	1.8	1.3
Livelihood strategies			
1	11.8	3.6	8.4
2	12.4	3.3	7.4
3	13.7	3.4	7.5
4	12.9	3.4	7.8
5	12.4	3.6	8.1

11.2   Gender and Household Type

In terms of the relationship between household type and food insecurity, it is clear that female-centred households are the worst off (Table 26). Female-centred households had a much higher mean HFIAS score (14.1) than the other household types included in this survey. Nuclear households had the lowest HFIAS at 11.9. Female-centred households also experienced the fewest months of food adequacy (7.3), especially compared to nuclear households (at 8.2). However, this relationship does not hold with regard to dietary diversity where female-centred households had more diverse diets than both male-centred and nuclear households. What this suggests is that when women have direct control over what money is spent on and what food is consumed within the household, they try to ensure a more diverse diet for household members. The relationship between gender and food security is confirmed when the sex of the household head is used as the independent variable. Female-headed households have worse HFIAS and HAHFP scores than male, but better dietary diversity.

11.3 Food Security and Social Protection

What is most striking is the relationship between food security and informal social protection. On all three indicators (borrowing food, sharing meals and obtaining food from other households), the vast majority of households were severely food insecure (Table 28). For example, 79% of those that borrowed food were severely food insecure. The figures were even higher (85%) for those that shared meals or obtained food from other households. Very few households that drew on these informal mechanisms to access food were food secure. Comparing these figures for the sample as a whole (where only 65% were severely food insecure), it is clear that informal social protection is the preserve of the most desperate but that access to food in this way certainly does not improve the overall food security status of the marginalized household. Unsurprisingly, therefore, the vast majority of these households have extremely low dietary diversity as well (Table 29).

TABLE 28: Informal Social Protection and Food Security

	Food secure (%)	Mildly food insecure (%)	Moderately food insecure (%)	Severely food insecure (%)	Total N
Shared meal with neighbours and/or other households	3	4	8	85	80
Food provided by neighbours and/or other households	3	3	9	85	102
Borrowed food from others	0	3	18	79	160

TABLE 29: Informal Social Protection and Dietary Diversity

	Household Dietary Diversity Score			
	<= 4 (%)	5-7 (%)	8+ (%)	Total N
Shared meal with neighbours and/or other households	91	5	4	78
Food provided by neighbours and/or other households	87	10	3	99
Borrowed food from others	81	17	1	156

12. HOUSEHOLD RESPONSES TO FOOD PRICE SHOCKS

This report has dwelt at some length on the food price crisis of 2007-2008 and the ways in which it was translated, via South Africa, into rapid increases in the market price of staples in Lesotho. Certainly, the long-term decline in agricultural production within the country and the drought of 2007 played a major in increasing household vulnerability in the rural areas. However, most households in Maseru now source the bulk of their food from supermarkets, small retail outlets and informal vendors and these suppliers, in turn, directly or indirectly source most of their produce from South Africa. In that respect, Maseru is no different from small towns and cities within South Africa itself. The question, then, is how the food price increase was experienced by households dependent on market sources for the bulk of their food and how they reacted to the shocks.

The vast majority of households reported a serious deterioration in their economic circumstances in the year prior to the survey: 75% said that they had got worse/much worse and only 9% that they had got better/much better (Table 30). Given that poor households in Maseru spend a large proportion of their income on food, it is not surprising that a dramatic increase in food prices would lead to strained economic circumstances as there would be less disposable income to spend on other necessities (Box 3). However, the crisis was so severe that many households were forced to go without food in the six months prior to the survey (Table 31). Only 6% of households reported that their food access was unaffected by food price increases. A quarter had gone without every day and nearly 50% had gone without at least once a week. In other words, even by adjusting household expenditure patterns, three-quarters of the surveyed households had regularly gone without food due to rising prices.

TABLE 30: Economic Condition of Households Compared to a Year Previously		
	No.	% of households
Much worse	367	47
Worse	224	28
Same	125	16
Better	68	9
Much better	2	0.3
Total	786	100.0

BOX 3: Food Price Shocks

Global food and fuel prices have increased significantly and Lesotho has not been an exception. Between January and July 2008, a market survey was carried (out) in ten district towns to determine changes in the prices and the differences between months... Both consumers and traders' perceptions were that prices increase significantly every month. The most impacted commodities... include maize meal, bread flour, vegetable oil, beans, rice and sugar while among the non-food commodities paraffin, candles, soap and gas were frequently mentioned. Traders felt that the rate at which consumers buy has declined significantly compared to the period prior to the price hikes. Consumers are not only purchasing smaller quantities but also prioritise only the basic commodities – most likely due to their declining purchasing power. This results in low profits in trade because sometimes traders wait to increase prices while they sensitise customers on future prices. This situation has prevailed despite the fact that the Government subsidised some basic commodities such as maize meal, pulses and milk which ended in April this year (2008). The impact of the increasing prices has been felt by all consumers although the most affected households are those who do not have economically productive members such as elderly headed households and those that host OVCs, poor households and households which depend mainly on petty trade, especially those living in urban areas. These households engage coping strategies such as relying on gifts, skipping meals, buying cheapest commodities, migrating to towns in search of jobs etc. Sometimes children in poor families skip school days because they do not have enough to eat.

Source: WFP/LVAC, "Vulnerability and Food Insecurity in Urban Areas of Lesotho" (2008), p. 7.

TABLE 31: Frequency of Going Without Food Due to Rising Food Prices in Previous Six Months

	No.	% of households
Every day	188	24
More than once a week but less than every day of the week	244	31
About once a week	127	16
About once a month	189	24
Never	49	6
Total	797	100

The answers to the HFIAS questions provide additional insights into what "going without food" actually meant to households. These questions asked respondents to reflect on their experience in the month prior to the survey (Table 32). The two types of food quantity indicators elicited very different responses, with absolute food shortages being less significant than reduced consumption. So, for example, the proportion of households that had often experienced a situation where there was no food to eat was 6-12%, depending on the indicator. However, the proportion who had often eaten fewer or smaller meals was 19-22%. At the other end of the spectrum, 40-61% of households had never experienced an absolute food shortage, whereas, by contrast, only 19-21% of households had never had to eat smaller or fewer meals. The impact of food insecurity on the food quality was much more direct and affected a large number of households. For example, around a third of households had often compromised on their food preferences and dietary diversity, while only 8-10% had never done so.

TABLE 32: Household Responses to Food Insecurity				
In the last month, did you:	Often (% of households)	Some-times (% of households)	Rarely (% of households)	Never (% of households)
Food quantity				
Eat smaller meals than you needed because there was not enough food?	22	35	24	19
Eat fewer meals in a day because there was not enough food?	19	33	26	22
Eat no food of any kind because of a lack of resources to obtain food?	12	20	29	40
Go to sleep hungry because there was not enough food?	7	16	22	55
Go a whole day and night without eating anything?	6	11	22	61
Food quality				
Not eat the kinds of foods you preferred because of a lack of resources?	33	29	30	8
Eat a limited variety of foods due to a lack of resources?	31	36	22	11
Eat foods you did not want because of a lack of resources to obtain other types of food?	33	35	22	10

As expected, low income households were disproportionately affected by the increased prices of food (Table 33). Of the poorest households in the lowest income tercile (<LSL 420), 80% said they went without food due to food price increases on at least a weekly basis, compared with 61% of households in the upper income tercile (=>LSL 1,000). Household food insecurity was also associated with sensitivity to food price increases.

Only 22% of households went without food at least once a week due to food price increases, compared to 31% of mildly food insecure households, 63% of moderately food insecure households and 80% of severely food insecure households. Of households that had not been affected by food price increases, 30% were categorized as food secure on the HFIAP. Amongst households affected by food prices on a daily basis, only 2% were food secure on the HFIAP. These findings indicate a close relationship between high food prices and household food insecurity in Maseru. Female-headed households were slightly more affected than male-headed households (76% versus 66% on at least a weekly basis). There were small differences in the effect of food prices on households of different sizes with larger households more vulnerable than smaller ones (30% versus 22% experiencing daily shortages).

TABLE 33: Frequency of Going Without Food Due to Price Increases		Never %	About once a month %	About once a week %	More than once a week %	Every day %	N
Household income	Poorest (<LSL420)	3	17	81	33	34	229
	Less poor (LSL420-999)	4	22	75	36	23	222
	Least poor (=>LSL1,000)	12	28	61	28	13	245
Household size	1-5	7	23	61	32	22	640
	6-10	2	28	70	26	30	151
	>10	0	17	83	50	33	6
Household head sex	Male	7	27	66	31	20	467
	Female	5	19	76	29	29	329
HFIAP	Food secure	41	38	3	8	11	37
	Mild insecurity	32	34	9	16	9	34
	Moderate insecurity	7	31	23	28	12	198
	Severe insecurity	1	19	15	35	30	511

Households were also asked which foods they had gone without due to food price increases in the previous six months. Top of the list was meat (three-quarters of households), followed by fish, milk products, oils/butter and fruit (all 50% or more). The inaccessibility of meats, fish and dairy is not surprising, given how resource intensive the production of meats and dairy are in comparison to grains or vegetables and how expensive meat and dairy products tend to be on the urban market. Cereals (maize and sorghum) are the major component of the diets of the poor, yet as many as 48% said that increased prices had meant that they had had to significantly reduce their consumption. The only food product that had not affected the vast majority of households was vegetables (only 22% had reduced their consumption due to price increases). This may well be because of the insulating effects of gardens in which households grew some of their own vegetables. Interestingly, as many as 55% of the households whose food access was not affected by food price increases relied on garden crops as a livelihood strategy.

TABLE 34: Types of Food Which Households Went Without Due to Price Increases		
	No.	% of households
Meat	554	74
Fish	501	67
Milk products	463	62
Oils/butter	461	62
Fruits	372	50
Grains	356	48
Eggs	349	47
Beans/nuts	327	44
Roots	307	41
Sugar/honey	298	40
Vegetables	162	22
Other foods	300	40
Note: More than one answer permitted		

The finding that the food price shocks of 2007–2008 were felt most keenly by the poorest and most food insecure households is confirmed by using the mean food security scores from the HFIAS, MAHFP and HDDS (Figures 20–22). Higher household frequency of going without due to food price increases was associated with higher (worse) mean HFIAS scores, lower (worse) mean MAHFP scores, and lower (worse) mean HDD scores. The quality of these relationships, however, was not consistently linear. While increased household frequency of going without food due to price increases was consistently related to higher mean HFIAS scores, there appeared to be a cut-off point in the HDD scores suggesting that the largest difference in dietary diversity occurs when a household went without food due to prices on a weekly basis or more frequently. That said, and as noted above, the HDDS scores were low for most households surveyed in Maseru.

The non-iterative nature of this investigation limits the inferences that can be made about household responses to the food price increases. However, categorizing household dependence on specific coping strategies by household frequency of going without food due to price increases can reveal patterns in coping strategy dependence based on food price impact. Among all households affected by food price, garden crops appear to be the most common coping strategy in Maseru. Household dependence on casual labour, self-employment and informal credit increases with frequency of going without food due to food price increases.

FIGURE 20: Mean HFIAS Score and Going Without Due to Food Price Increases

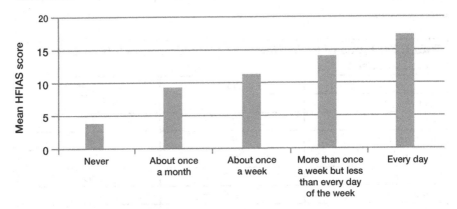

FIGURE 21: Mean MAHFP Score and Going Without Due to Food Price Increases

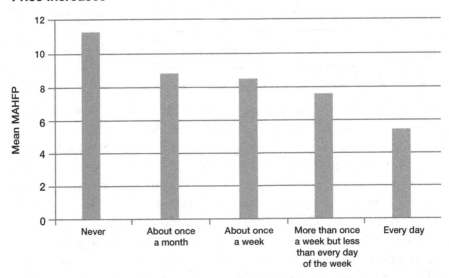

FIGURE 22: Mean HDD Score and Going Without Due to Food Price Increases

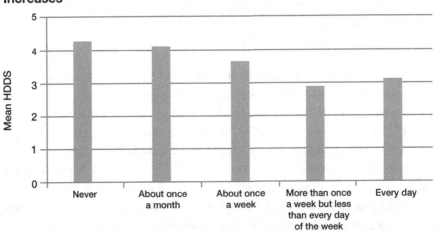

13. CONCLUSION

Perhaps the most striking outcome of the AFSUN surveys is the consistency in levels of food insecurity amongst the urban poor in all 11 SADC cities. The depth of food insecurity closely reflects the depth of poverty in which urbanites live in Southern Africa.[109] Maseru is no exception and it therefore comes as no surprise that 60-70% of poor households surveyed were severely food insecure. While food price increases worsen food insecurity for poor households, it is poverty that weakens the resilience of society to absorb these increases. Within the context of persistent and rising poverty and hunger, this report argues that Maseru residents face specific and interrelated challenges with respect to food and nutrition insecurity. These are:

1. Poverty;

2. Limited local livelihood opportunities; and

3. Dependence on food imports.

All three factors increase the vulnerability of the urban poor to food and nutrition insecurity and are interrelated, which points to the need to consider policy options that promote integrated approaches to addressing chronic hunger. Typically, and as demonstrated in this report, food security is seen as synonymous with domestic agricultural development in Lesotho, evidenced by the positioning of food security within the Ministry of Agriculture and Food Security.

A productionist view of food security in a rapidly urbanizing country like Lesotho ignores the evidence presented in this paper, which demonstrates that simply increasing farm yields will do little to reduce the vulnerabilities associated with poverty and limited livelihoods. Furthermore, the third vulnerability – dependence on food imports – will also not be ameliorated through increased agricultural production because 99% of Lesotho's retail food is embedded in complex supermarket value chains that are integrated into South African agribusiness.[110] The more likely outcome of an increase in commercially viable agricultural yields will be opportunities for export into the dominant South African value chain, with little trickle-down to the majority of the urban or rural poor. With only about 10% of land suitable for crop production, local small-scale farmers are unlikely to compete effectively with South African agriculture.[111] Given the trilogy of vulnerabilities that characterize food insecurity in Maseru (and within the country more broadly), what kinds of policies are then available to improve food and nutrition security amongst the urban poor in Lesotho? The remainder of this report outlines the foundations of a suggested integrated urban food security strategy for Maseru.

13.1   Proposed Integrated Food Security Strategy

Four-Pillar Approach

All too often food security is seen as a discrete development objective, as a condition to be alleviated through actions that target food itself. The result is a series of approaches that focus on increasing food production, which, as is argued here and elsewhere in the AFSUN policy series and more broadly in the food security literature, does not translate into improved urban food security at the household level.[112] Lesotho's supermarkets are not short of food; yet at least 60-70% of Maseru households do not have adequate access to that food. This paradox of hunger amidst plenty is neither the product of a strained food supply system nor is it unique to Maseru. Indeed, the heart of the matter rests not within the specific area of food security, but rather within socio-economic development, more broadly conceived. For example, a study of food riots in Cameroon found that food itself was a background factor and that the civil unrest was better explained by widespread dissatisfaction with poor levels of urban development and services and the precarious lives that these conditions create and perpetuate.[113]

The approach advocated here therefore focuses on development priorities and views food security as a development outcome. In other words, improvements in food security will happen when broader development needs are met. Recent analyses of urban food security data support a view that improvements in food security may be best achieved when policy targets development priorities.[114] This approach considers food security to be a proxy indicator for societal development needs, and is based on the following four pillars:

- Infrastructure
- Livelihoods
- Welfare
- Mobility

Infrastructure Development

Access to physical and social infrastructure appears to be a particularly strong predictor of food security, even stronger than access to income.[115] Tacoli et al. argue that "inadequate housing and basic infrastructure and limited access to services contribute to levels of malnutrition and food insecurity that are often as high if not higher than in rural areas."[116] While these findings might be surprising to policy makers and development planners, they offer (1) a partial explanation as to why increases in food supply do not translate directly into improvements in household food security; and (2) a way to provide a broader range of improvements in people's lives, one of which would be increased food security.

While access to infrastructure is increasingly being recognized as a critical dimension of development and food and nutrition security, the provision of urban infrastructure in Maseru has fallen behind the growth of the city. The need for decent bulk infrastructure is high. While data for rural and urban areas is difficult to find, Lesotho is considered to have one of the lowest levels of access to electricity for its population (less than 10%). Electricity costs are also amongst the highest in Sub-Saharan Africa.[117] Water access is much more widespread than electricity; however, it is estimated that less than three percent of urban households have access to sanitation infrastructure.[118]

These figures support the argument that rapid urbanization demands significant and ongoing investment in infrastructure. Research is clear that the quality of urban infrastructure is a key component of households' resilience to shocks, especially as houses and their related environments are often productive assets and are used as the basis of livelihood strategies by the poor.[119] Case studies from cities in Southern Africa demonstrate that high levels of informality in the urban fabric in poor neighbourhoods translates into increased vulnerability to food insecurity, particularly in relation to housing, water and electricity, all of which are key productive assets.[120] Focusing on this as a development priority not only means the potential for improvements in levels of infrastructure access for urban households, but will also be instrumental in reducing levels of food insecurity amongst poor and underserviced households.

Improving Livelihoods Opportunities

Income generation is the basis of livelihoods in towns and cities. There needs to be a focus on improving livelihoods as a basis for increasing household access to food, with an emphasis on increasing participation within the food system itself. The food system provides an excellent opportunity to increase livelihood opportunities in Maseru. This report has described the proliferation of the informal economy in the area known as CBD East, where informal traders sell a range of goods, including fruit, vegetables and other types of food. However, informal activities in Maseru are constrained by heavy policing as town planning and health bylaws make informal activities illegal, particularly with regard to the food sector.[121] Notwithstanding existing land use regulations that stifle the informal economy, the limited opportunities for wage employment in the formal economy highlight the importance and potential of informality as an economic and livelihood conduit for the urban poor and the unemployed. Permitting greater participation in the informal sector should therefore be a policy priority for the city; this has been done elsewhere with positive livelihood and food security outcomes.[122]

More specifically, food itself has the potential to be used as a livelihood strategy. With rapid urbanization, supporting food production in Maseru may provide significant business opportunities for small-scale urban and peri-urban farming. However, with almost all food in the city being supplied by supermarkets, policy will have to support local suppliers and assist in integrating them into the existing value chain. The major supermarket chains are already involved in community-based farming as one supply avenue for high-value produce. For example, some South African supermarket chains are beginning to be more engaged with small-scale farmers in South Africa and elsewhere on the continent. Motivated more by corporate social responsibility and political considerations than sheer profit, this does provide some leverage for local suppliers. An example of the commitment of supermarkets to a locally-focused supply chain is evident in Pick n Pay's principles as follows:

- Sustained capacity-building for small-scale farmers and other entrepreneurs in order to improve their competitiveness.
- Entrepreneurs taking advantage of collective action, either as co-operatives, producer organizations or other forms of association.
- Collaboration between the public and the private sectors in terms of linking small enterprises to formal markets.
- Increasing the number of small-scale farmers who have access to larger retail markets.
- The provision of mentors (preferably retired Pick n Pay executives and successful business people) who are assigned as decision-making support to small-scale entrepreneurs to ensure the limitation of punitive mistakes.[123]

With the right policy environment, and given relatively high rates of participation in urban farming, this experience could be transferable to Maseru.[124] Leveraging these kinds of commitments from the large supermarket chains would provide tangible livelihood opportunities for farmers, processors and retailers to supply both the formal supermarkets and the local (formal and informal) food system entrepreneurs. Improving market opportunities within the food sector for the urban poor in Maseru would in turn raise the incomes of farmers and urban residents, which would enhance local buying power. This would benefit formal and informal businesses and livelihoods in the city (and potentially in the rural areas if Lesotho agriculture were to be a part of the strategy).

Welfare and Social Safety Nets

The Lesotho Government has recognized the need to improve health and social welfare service coverage in the country, and that there is a direct link between poverty and health and social problems. In addition, it has had to prioritize the care of orphans as a result of the high AIDS-related mortality rate in the country.[125] These efforts are laudable and are an important contribution to the country's pro-poor development. As a related social welfare strategy, the government has introduced a range of other social protection mechanisms in recent years. A state pension is now available to citizens from the age of 70 years and is proving to be a valuable strategy in the fight against poverty amongst the elderly. Benefits were observed after only two years of the pension scheme coming into effect. As one commentator observed, it is "a meager amount, but it has brought an end to backbreaking toil and food insecurity for many of Lesotho's elderly."[126]

The Child Grants Programme (CGP) started in 2009 as a donor-funded initiative. By 2014, the Ministry of Social Development had enrolled 20,000 poor means-tested, mainly rural, households and 50,000 children who receive between LSL360 and LSL750 per quarter (covering 40% of eligible households). An evaluation of the programme noted that it "has had positive impacts in areas related to programme objectives, particularly on child wellbeing."[127] Amongst the key findings were that the CGP (a) raised incomes but did not significantly decrease the overall poverty of households; (b) increased household spending on children's education and clothing and (c) improved the ability of households to access food throughout the year. Amongst the recommendations of the evaluation was the following: "as the programme also expands to urban areas it would be necessary to consider its potential role and design adaptations required to tackle vulnerabilities that are specific to the urban poor."

There is a well-established literature on social protection and its positive impacts on poverty alleviation and food and nutrition security, especially for children and other vulnerable groups.[128] In Lesotho, the depth of poverty and food insecurity affects far more people than those who are eligible for the old-age pension. The experiences of countries elsewhere demonstrate the positive value of extending old-age pensions to those younger than 70 and including the poor and most vulnerable in universal social protection programmes. Often the costs associated with expanded social safety nets are cited as the main constraint to their provision. However, the benefits are significant in that they do promote economic growth, an important development objective for Lesotho.[129] This works through six channels:

- Social safety nets help create individual, household and community assets;
- They help households protect assets when shocks occur;
- By helping households cope with risk, they permit households to use their existing resources more effectively;
- They increase consumer spending especially on basic necessities such as food clothing, health and education;
- They facilitate structural reforms to the economy; and
- By reducing inequality, they directly raise growth rates.[130]

Social safety net mechanisms for consideration in the context of Lesotho include (1) transfers; and (2) asset building. Conditional and unconditional cash and/or food transfers have been used with success in a variety of situations. These involve direct payments or food transfers to vulnerable groups and can be done on a means-tested basis. These programmes help to alleviate acute and chronic food insecurity and should be considered as part of a total welfare package. An important instrument here is the CGP, which has the potential to markedly decrease the vulnerability of children to food insecurity.[131] Given the number of children in Maseru and other urban centres, this would be a critical intervention. The second approach – asset building – is a longer-term strategy that aims to reduce poverty and vulnerability through livelihood support, and links directly to the other pillars of this strategy. Welfare (and associated social safety nets) is an important dimension of any poverty-reducing strategy, and realistic, proven policies and programmes need to be explored and adapted to the context of Lesotho and Maseru.

Mobility

Lesotho is not an island, however much donors and national development plans appear to imagine it is. Over the years it has made a major contribution to the industrialization and economic growth of South Africa through the blood and sweat of its people. The most recent LDS survey found that there were over 120,000 Basotho still working in South Africa, which is probably a conservative estimate. While the skilled and educated can obtain work permits relatively easily, the same does not apply to the semi-skilled and unskilled. The numbers of legal Basotho mineworkers continue to decline not because the mines do not want them (Basotho are highly-valued employees) but because the South African government is making it more difficult to employ foreign migrants. So the unemployed cross the border and work clandestinely in various risky and low-paid jobs such as commercial farmwork, construction, domestic service and illegal mining. They are unprotected by South African labour legislation and easily abused and exploited by employers. Informal traders involved in cross-border trade, especially women, also face a host of obstacles, inconveniences and added financial costs at border posts.[132] The quickest and most effective way to increase incomes, reduce poverty and address food insecurity in Lesotho would be to open the borders and allow Basotho to work and trade legally in South Africa. This was the implicit understanding between the two governments in a 2004 bilateral agreement between the two countries. The full implementation of this agreement would immediately increase the financial resources of many Basotho households, and with it their levels of food security.

In summary, this report has proposed a four-pillar development strategy that has the potential to improve food and nutrition security across the city in Maseru. We have argued that:

- Improved infrastructure is a fundamental pre-condition for meaningful development;

- Good infrastructure is associated with improved livelihood and food security outcomes;

- The food system itself has significant potential to open up livelihood opportunities across the value chain, specifically with the support of the major supermarkets, which dominate the food sector;

- An enabling policy environment is needed to facilitate the growth of the informal sector as a livelihoods strategy;

- There is a need to provide at least a minimum of welfare support (social safety nets) for chronically poor households, which will improve food security outcomes for individuals and households, especially for children;

- Social safety nets can be designed and implemented in ways that promote economic growth and equity; and

- Free movement of labour between Lesotho and South Africa would dramatically improve the food security of many poor households.

The Government of Lesotho and the Maseru Municipality and District can direct both aid and investment into an integrated food security strategy that prioritizes urban infrastructure, livelihoods, welfare and mobility. This takes political will, but the development and implementation of such a food security strategy is well within the reach of the country's leaders.

ENDNOTES

1   "Lesotho: Weather Extremes Threaten Food Security" *IRIN News* 24 February 2012; "Lesotho: Food Security Goes from Bad to Worse" *IRIN News* 26 June 2012; K. Patel, "Lesotho: A Slow Descent Into Starvation: *Daily Maverick* 30 June 2012; M. Tran, "Lesotho: Hungry and Largely Forgotten as Donor Pledges Ring Hollow" *The Guardian* 29 November 2012.

2   International Red Cross and Red Crescent Societies, "Lesotho: Sustainable Food Security Practices" Geneva, nd, p. 1.

3   "Declaration of an Emergency on Food Security in Lesotho, August 2012" at http://www.gov.ls/documents/speeches/declaration%20food%20insecurity%20 20122013[1].pdf

4   J. Crush and B. Frayne, "Feeding African Cities: The Growing Challenge of Urban Food Insecurity" In S. Parnell and E. Pieterse, eds., *Africa's Urban Revolution* (London: Zed Books, 2014), pp. 110-32.

5   World Food Programme/LVAC, *Vulnerability and Food Insecurity in Urban Areas of Lesotho* (Rome: WFP, 2008).

6   J. Crush and O. Namasasu, "Rural Rehabilitation in the Basotho Labour Reserve" *Applied Geography* 5(1985): 83-98; T. Sambaiwe and T. Makatsiane, "Migration and Rural Crisis in a Labour Reserve Economy: Lesotho" In M. Toure and T. Fadayomi, eds., *Migrations, Development and Urbanization Policies in Sub-Saharan Africa* (Dakar: CODESRIA, 1992), pp. 237-76; J. Cobbe, " Lesotho: From Labor Reserve to Depopulating Periphery?" Migration Policy Institute, Washington DC, 2012.

7   R. Leduka, "Lesotho Urban Land Market Scoping Study" Report for Urban LandMark, ISAS, Roma, 2012, p. 2.

8   http://www.un.org/en/development/desa/population/publications/pdf/ urbanization/2007_urban_rural_chart.pdf

9   D. Ambrose, *Maseru: An Illustrated History* (Morija, 1993).

10 S. Romaya and A. Brown, "City Profile: Maseru, Lesotho" *Cities* 16(1999): 123-33.

11 Ibid.

12 R. Leduka and S. Sets'abi, "The Politics of Street Trading in Maseru, Lesotho" *Urban Forum* 19(2008): 221-41.

13 Ibid.

14 WFP/LVAC, *Vulnerability and Food Insecurity in Urban Areas of Lesotho*.

15 D. Croome, M. Molisana and A. Nyanguru, "Impact of the Old Age Pension on Hunger and Vulnerability: A Case Study from the Mountain Zone of Lesotho" Institute for Southern African Studies, National University of Lesotho, Roma, 2007; P. Maro, *Environmental Change in Lesotho* (London: Springer, 2011); C. Matarira, E. Shava, E. Pedzisai and D. Manatsa, "Food Insecurity in Mountain Communities of Lesotho" *Journal of Hunger & Environmental Nutrition* 9(2014): 280-96.

16 K. Thabane, B. Honu and C. Paramiah, "Determinants of Household-Level Vulnerability to Poverty in Mohale's Hoek District, Lesotho" *International NGO Journal* 9(2014): 17-25.

17   L. Marais, "Urbanisation, Urban Dilemmas and Urban Challenges in Lesotho" *Acta Academia* 33(2001): 88-109.

18   J. Crush, B. Dodson, J. Gay, T. Green and C. Leduka, *Migration, Remittances and 'Development' in Lesotho*, SAMP Migration Policy Series No. 52, Cape Town, 2010.

19   P. Gwimbi, T. Thomas, S. Hachigonta and L. Sibanda, "Lesotho" In S. Hachigonta, G. Nelson, T. Thomas and L. Sibanda, eds., *Southern African Agriculture and Climate Change: A Comprehensive Analysis* (Washington DC: IFPRI, 2013), p. 84.

20   M. Moeletsi and S. Walker, "Agroclimatological Suitability Mapping for Dryland Maize Production in Lesotho" *Theoretical and Applied Climatology*, 114(2013): 227-36.

21   E. Obioha, "Climate Variability and Food Production Nexus in Lesotho, 2001-2007" *Journal of Human Ecology* 32(2010): 149-60.

22   FAO/WFP, *Crop and Food Supply Assessment Mission to Lesotho: Special Report* (Rome, 2005); Obioha, "Climate Variability and Food Production Nexus in Lesotho"; Disaster Management Authority, *Lesotho Rural Livelihoods: Baseline Profiles* (Maseru, 2012).

23   Matarira et al. "Food Insecurity in Mountain Communities of Lesotho."

24   J. Dewbre and B. David, "A Note on the 2011 Lesotho Child Grants Program (CGP) Baseline Data" Report for FAO, Rome, 5 October 2012, p. 5.

25   Bureau of Statistics, *Foreign Trade Statistics Report 2009* (Maseru, 2012), p. 69.

26   B. Mukeere and S. Dradri, *Food Aid, Food Production and Food Markets in Lesotho: An Analytical Review* (Rome: FAO, 2006).

27   Bureau of Statistics, *Lesotho Utilization and Availability of Cereals 2011/2012*, Statistical Report No. 26/2012, Maseru, p. 9.

28   World Bank, "World Development Indicators" 2014.

29   Ibid.

30   Marais, "Urbanisation, Urban Dilemmas, and Urban Challenges in Lesotho."

31   S. Turner and M. Adams, "A Note on Food Security and Land Tenure Security in Lesotho" at http://www.mokoro.co.uk/files/13/publication/P1161-adams_Lesotho_Dec2004.pdf

32   World Bank, "Agricultural Sector Assessment and Agribusiness Development Strategy" at http://siteresources.worldbank.org/INTLESOTHO/Resources/Agric_Policy_Note_Lesotho.pdf

33   Ibid.

34   L. Mphahama, "Institutional Constraints to Horticulture Production and Marketing in Lesotho" M.Ag.Econ. Thesis, Fort Hare University, 2011.

35   FEWS NET, "Lesotho Desk Review October 2013" at http://fews.org/docs/Publications/LS_DeskReview_2013_10.pdf

36   World Bank, "Agricultural Sector Assessment."

37   Ibid.

38   World Bank. "World Development Indicators." World Development Indicators Database, World DataBank, 2014.

39   A. de Waal and A. Whiteside, "New Variant Famine?: AIDS and Food Crisis in Southern Africa" *Lancet* 362(2003): 1234-7.

40   M. Daemane, "The Review of Urbanization Process and Local Governance Implications on Sustainable Urban-Human Development and Poverty Reduction: Pragmatic Views on Lesotho" *Journal of Sustainable Development in Africa* 16(2014): 97-112.

41   http://www.unep.org/eou/Portals/52/Reports/CC_Lesotho_ExecSummary.html

42   http://www.unicef.org.uk/UNICEFs-Work/What-we-do/Issues-we-work-on/Climate-change/Climate-adaptation-case-studies/Lesotho/

43   M. Malebajoa, "Climate Change Impacts on Crop Yields and Adaptive Measures for Agricultural Sector in the Lowlands of Lesotho" MA Thesis, Lund University, 2010.

44   G. Ziervogel and R. Calder, "Climate Variability and Rural Livelihoods: Assessing the Impact of Seasonal Climate Forecasts in Lesotho" *Area* 35(2003): 403-17; J. Bell, "'The Changing Climate of Livelihoods in Lesotho': The Vulnerability of Rural Livelihoods in Phelantaba Village, Northern Lesotho, to Climate variability and Change" MA Thesis, University of Johannesburg, 2012; C. Matarira, D. Pullanikkatil, T. Kaseke, E. Shava and D. Manatsa, "Socio-Economic Impacts of Climate Change on Subsistence Communities: Some Observations from Lesotho" *International Journal of Climate Change Strategies and Management* 5(2013): 404-17; T. Sekaleli and K. Sebusi, "Farmers' Response and Adaptation Strategies to Climate Change in Mafeteng District, Lesotho" WP 74, African Technology Policy Studies Network, Nairobi, 2013.

45   C. Matarira, D. Pullanikkatil, T. Kaseke, E. Shava and D. Manatsa, "Socio-Economic Impacts of Climate Change on Subsistence Communities: Some Observations from Lesotho" *International Journal of Climate Change Strategies and Management* 5(2013): 404-17; S. Gwimbi, T. Thomas, S. Hachigonta and L. Sibanda, "Lesotho" In S. Hachigonta, G. Nelson, T. Thomas and L. Sibanda, eds., *Southern African Agriculture and Climate Change: A Comprehensive Analysis* (Washington DC: IFPRI, 2013), pp. 71-110.

46   S. Gwimbi, S. Hachigonta, L. Sibanda and T. Thomas, "Southern African Agriculture and Climate Change: A Comprehensive Analysis - Lesotho" Report for IFPRI, Washington, 2012.

47   Turner, "Promoting Food Security in Lesotho: Issues and Options 2009, p. 21.

48   FAO, *FAOSTAT*. Rome, 2012.

49   Mukeere and Dradri, *Food Aid, Food Production and Food Markets in Lesotho*.

50   Bureau of Statistics, *Foreign Trade Statistics Report 2011* (Maseru, 2014), pp. 5-6.

51   J. Clapp and M. Cohen, eds., *The Global Food Crisis: Governance Challenges and Opportunities* (Waterloo: WLU Press, 2009).

52   M. Cohen and M. Smale, eds., *Global Food-Price Shocks and Poor People: Themes and Case Studies* (London: Routledge, 2012); N. Minot, "Transmission of World Food Price Changes to Markets in Sub-Saharan Africa Markets" Working Paper No. 01059, International Food Policy Research Institute, 2011; F. Cachia, "Regional Food Price Inflation Transmission" ESS Working Paper 14-01, Food and Agriculture Organization, Rome, 2014.

53   M. Verpoorten, A. Arora, N. Stoop and J. Swinnen, "Self-Reported Food Insecurity in Africa During the Food Price Crisis" *Food Policy* 39(2013): 51-63.

54   *The 2007-2008 Food Price Swing Impact and Policies in Eastern and Southern Africa* (Rome: FAO, 2008); T. Jayne, A. Chapoto, I. Minde and C. Donovan, "The

2008/09 Food Price and Food Security Situation in Eastern and Southern Africa" MSU International Development Working Paper No. 97, Michigan State University, East Lansing, 2008; G. Rapsomaniikis, "The 2007-2008 Food Price Episode: Impact and Policies in Eastern and Southern Africa" FAO Commodities and Trade Technical Paper No. 12, Rome, 2009.

55   J. Kirsten, "The Political Economy of Food Price Policy in South Africa" Working Paper No. 2012/102, UNU-WIDER, 2012, p. 7.

56   Ibid., p. 8.

57   Ibid., p. 9.

58   L. Rangasamy, "Food Inflation in South Africa: Some Implications for Economic Policy" *South African Journal of Economics* 79(2011): 184-201.

59   Kirsten, "Political Economy of Food Price Policy in South Africa."

60   Ibid., p. 17.

61   Ibid., pp. 15-18.

62   M. Nchake, L. Edwards and N. Rankin, "Price Setting Behaviour in Lesotho: Stylised Facts from Consumer Retail Prices" Working Paper No. 417, Economic Research Southern Africa, 2014.

63   R. Thamae and M. Letsoela, "Food Inflation in Lesotho: Implications for Monetary Policy" *African Review of Economics and Finance* 6(2014): 56-68.

64   Central Bank of Lesotho, *The Impact of Food Prices on Overall Inflation in Lesotho*, 2007 (Maseru, 2007).

65   M. Ruel, J. Garrett, C. Hawkes and M. Cohen, "The Food, Fuel, and Financial Crises Affect the Urban and Rural Poor Disproportionately: A Review of the Evidence" *Journal of Nutrition* 140(2010): 170S-6S; G. Anríquez, S. Daidone and E. Mane, "Rising Food Prices and Undernourishment: A Cross-Country Inquiry" *Food Policy* 38(2013): 190-202.

66   R. Bush, "Food Riots: Poverty, Power and Protest" *Journal of Agrarian Change* 10(2010): 119-29; J. Berezneva and D. Lee, "Explaining the African Food Riots of 2007-2008: An Empirical Analysis" *Food Policy* 39(2013): 28-39.

67   Berezneva and Lee, "Explaining the African Food Riots."

68   M. Cohen and J. Garrett, "The Food Price Crisis and Urban Food (In)security" *Environment and Urbanization* 22(2010): 467-82.

69   Ibid., p. 467.

70   Ibid., p. 473.

71   Leduka, "Lesotho Urban Land Market Scoping Study"; V. Thebe and M. Rakotje, "Land Strategies and Livelihood Dynamics in Peri-urban Communities: Challenges to Land and Agricultural Policy in Lesotho" *African Studies* 72(2013): 399-415.

72   J. Coates, A. Swindale and P. Bilinsky, "Household Food Insecurity Access Scale (HFIAS) for Measurement of Food Access: Indicator Guide (Version 3)" Food and Nutrition Technical Assistance Project, Academy for Educational Development, Washington DC, 2007.

73   Ibid.

74   A. Swindale and P. Bilinsky, "Household Dietary Diversity Score (HDDS) for Measurement of Household Food Access: Indicator Guide (Version 2)" Food and

Nutrition Technical Assistance Project, Academy for Educational Development, Washington DC, 2006.

75   P. Bilinsky and A. Swindale, "Months of Adequate Household Food Provisioning (MAHFP) for Measurement of Household Food Access: Indicator Guide" Food and Nutrition Technical Assistance Project, Academy for Educational Development, Washington DC, 2007.

76   S. Lall, "FDI, AGOA and Manufactured Exports by a Landlocked, Least Developed African Economy: Lesotho" *Journal of Development Studies* 41(2005): 998-1022.

77   P. Gibbon, "AGOA, Lesotho's 'Clothing Miracle' and the Politics of Sweatshops" *Review of African Political Economy* 30 (2003): 315-50; G. Seidman, "Labouring Under an Illusion: Lesotho's 'Sweat-Free' Label" *Third World Quarterly* 30(2009): 581-98.

78   G. Mills, "Lesotho's Textile Industry Unravels" Brenthurst Foundation News Release, 11 September 2011.

79   P. Gibbon, "AGOA, Lesotho's 'Clothing Miracle' and the Politics of Sweatshops" *Review of African Political Economy* 30 (2003): 315-50; G. Seidman, "Labouring Under an Illusion: Lesotho's 'Sweat-Free' Label" *Third World Quarterly* 30(2009): 581-98.

80   S. Mensah and V. Naidoo, "Migration Shocks: Integrating Lesotho's Retrenched Migrant Miners" *International Migration Review* 45(2011): 1017-42; S. Mensah, "The Impact of Dwindling Opportunities for Mine Migration on Rural Household Income in Lesotho" *Studies in Economics and Econometrics* 36(2012): 25-46; N. Nalane, A. Chikanda and J. Crush, *The Remittances Framework in Lesotho: Assessment of Policies and Programmes Promoting the Multiplier Effect*, Report for ACP Migration Observatory, Brussels, 2012.

81   L. Griffin, "Borderwork: 'Illegality', Un-bounded Labour and the Lives of Basotho Domestic Workers" PhD Thesis, University of Melbourne, 2010; L. Griffin, "Unravelling Rights: 'Illegal' Migrant Domestic Workers in South Africa" *South African Review of Sociology* 42(2011): 83-101; L. Griffin, "When Borders Fail" 'Illegal' Invisible Labour Migration and Basotho Domestic Workers in South Africa" In E. Guild and S. Mantu, eds., *Constructing and Imagining Labour Migration* (Farnham: Ashgate, 2011), pp.15-38.

82   N. Waterman, "Commercial Sex Workers: Adult Education and Pathways out of Poverty" at http://www.docstoc.com/docs/164676907/Commercial-sex-workers-adult-education-and-pathways-out-of-poverty

83   Ibid.

84   T. Makepe, N. Waterman and Y. Pencheliah, "Commercial Sex Work in Lesotho: An Issue of Social Justice" In M. Mapetla, A. Schlyter and B. Bless, eds., *Urban Experiences of Gender, Generations and Social Justice* (Roma: ISAS, 2007): 165-92.

85   WFP/LVAC, *Vulnerability and Food Insecurity in Urban Areas of Lesotho*.

86   Ibid., p. 13.

87   M. Mphale, "HIV/AIDS and Food Insecurity in Lesotho" at http://www.sarpn.org.za/documents/d0000222/mphale/Lesotho_food_security.pdf

88   Bureau of Statistics, *Lesotho Agricultural Census Volume III - Urban: Crops and Livestock Statistics* (Maseru, 2009/10).

89   M. Daemane and K. Mot'soene, "Transactional Loss of Land Threatening

Sustainable Development of Livelihoods in Urban Maseru" *Journal of Sustainable Development in Africa* 14(2012): 132-44; Thebe and Rakotje, "Land Strategies and Livelihood Dynamics in Peri-urban Communities".

90   Bureau of Statistics and FAO, *Lesotho Agricultural Census Volume III-Urban: Crops and Livestock Statistics,* Maseru, 1999/2000. Table A16.

91   J. Crush, A. Hovorka and D. Tevera, "Food Security in Southern African Cities: The Place of Urban Agriculture" *Progress in Development Studies* 11(2011): 285-305.

92   Bureau of Statistics, *Lesotho Urban Agriculture Report 2008/2009*, Maseru, 2010; Bureau of Statistics, *Lesotho Urban Agriculture Report 2011/2012*. Maseru, 2013.

93   Ibid.

94   Ibid.

95   R. Leduka, "Contested Urban Space: The Local State vs. Street Traders in Maseru's CBD West" Paper Presented to a Nordic Africa Institute Workshop on Urban Governance, Gender and Markets, Bamako, Mali, 2002.

96   S. Sets'abi, "Public Space and Livelihoods in Maseru" at http://www.cf.ac.uk/cplan/mls/setsabi_fieldwork.pdf

97   Sets'abi and Leduka, "Politics of Street Trading in Maseru."

98   T. Seeiso, "Bacteriological Quality of Meat in Lesotho" MSc Thesis, University of Pretoria; 2009; T. Seeiso and C. McCrindle, " An Investigation of the Quality of Meat Sold in Lesotho" *Journal of the South African Veterinary Association* 80(2009): 237-42.

99   S. Hanisch, "South-South Migration: The Case of Chinese Migrants in Lesotho" MA Thesis, University of Vienna, 2012; S. Hanisch, "At the Margins of the Economy? Chinese Migrants in Lesotho's Wholesale and Retail Sector" *Africa Spectrum* 48(2013): 85-97.

100   Hanisch, "At the Margins of the Economy", p. 91.

101   Ibid., p. 90.

102   S. Hanisch, "South-South Migration."

103   M. Olivier, "Social Protection in Lesotho: Innovations and Reform Challenges" *Development Southern Africa* 30(2013): 98-110.

104   P. Gwimbi, "Social Protection and Climate Change Adaptation in Lesotho: Opportunities and Constraints" In S. Devereux and M. Getu, eds., *Informal and Formal Social Protection Systems in Sub-Saharan Africa* (Kampala: Fountain Publishers, 2013), p. 170.

105   S. Turner, "Livelihoods and Sharing: Trends in a Lesotho Village, 1976-2004" PLAAS Research Report No. 22, University of the Western Cape, 2005.

106   Ibid., p. xi.

107   W. Pendleton, J. Crush and N. Nickanor, "Migrant Windhoek: Rural-Urban Migration and Food Security in Namibia" *Urban Forum* 25(2014):191-205.

108   M. Ranneileng, "Impact of a Nutrition education Intervention on Nutritional Status and Nutrition-Related Knowledge, Attitudes, Beliefs and Practices of Basotho Women in Urban and Rural Areas in Lesotho" Ph.D. Thesis, Free State University, 2013.

109   B. Frayne et al. *The State of Urban Food Insecurity in Southern Africa*. AFSUN Urban Food Security Series No. 2, Cape Town, 2010.

110   J. Crush and B. Frayne, "Supermarket Expansion and the Informal Food

Economy in Southern African Cities: Implications for Urban Food Security" *Journal of Southern African Studies* 37(2011): 781-807.

111 World Bank, "Agricultural Sector Assessment."

112 R. Sonnino, "Feeding the City: Towards a New Research and Planning Agenda" *International Planning Studies* 14(2009): 425-35; B. Frayne, C. McCordic and H. Shilomboleni, "Assessing Contributions of Urban Agriculture to Household Food Security in Southern African Cities" *Urban Forum* 25 (2014): 177-98; B. Frayne, J. Crush and M. McLachlan "Urbanization, Nutrition and Development in Southern African Cities" *Food Security* 6(2014): 101-12; Crush and Frayne, "Feeding African Cities."

113 L. Sneyd, "Evaluating the Contributions of Wild Foods to Food Security in Urban Cameroon" PhD Thesis, University of Guelph, 2014.

114 T. Ogun, "Infrastructure and Poverty Reduction: Implications for Urban Development in Nigeria" WIDER Working Paper No. 43, World Institute for Development Economics Research, Helsinki, 2010; D. Rose, J. Bodor, P. Hutchinson and C. Swalm, "The Importance of a Multi-Dimensional Approach for Studying the Links between Food Access and Consumption" *Journal of Nutrition* 140(2010): 1170-74.

115 B. Frayne and C. McCordic, "Planning for Food Secure Cities: Measuring the Influence of Infrastructure and Income on Household Food Security in Southern African Cities" Draft AFSUN Report, University of Waterloo, Waterloo, 2014.

116 C. Tacoli, B. Bukhari and S. Fisher, "Urban Poverty, Food Security and Climate Change" Human Settlements Working Paper 37, IIED, 2013, p. iv.

117 Z. Bogeti, "International Benchmarking of Lesotho's Infrastructure Performance" Policy Research Working Paper 3825, World Bank, Washington DC, 2006.

118 P. Monongoaha, "Challenges of Urbanisation for Sanitation Infrastructure in Lesotho" at http://capacity4dev.ec.europa.eu/public-water_and_sanitation/document/challenges-urbanisation-sanitation-infrastructure-lesotho

119 C. Moser, A. Norton, A. Stein and S. Georgieva, "Pro-Poor Adaptation to Climate Change in Urban Centres: Case Study of Vulnerability and Resilience in Kenya and Nicaragua" Report No. 54947-GLB, World Bank, Washington DC, 2010.

120 B. Frayne, C. Moser and G. Ziervogel, eds., *Climate Change, Assets and Food Security in Southern African Cities* (London: Earthscan, 2012).

121 Leduka and Sets'abi, "Politics of Street Trading in Maseru"; P. Tanga, *Informal Sector and Poverty: The Case of Street Vendors in Lesotho* (Addis Ababa: OSSREA, 2009); K. Mots'oene, "The Informal Sector and Human Capacity Building for Sustainable Development in Maseru" *Journal of Emerging Trends in Economics and Management Sciences* 7(2014): 109-14.

122 C. Rocha and I. Lessa, "Urban Governance for Food Security: The Alternative Food System in Belo Horizonte, Brazil" *International Planning Studies* 14 (2009): 389-400.

123 http://www.picknpay.co.za/foundation

124 http://www.woolworths.co.za/store/fragments/corporate/corporate-index.jsp?content=corporate-landing&contentId=fol110080

125 http://www.health.gov.ls/

126 http://mg.co.za/article/2006-11-03-lesotho-pension-system-proves-sceptics-

wrong; M. Daemane and K. Mots'oene, "Lessons on Old Age Pensions as Welfare Investment for Sustainable Development in Lesotho" *Journal of Emerging Trends in Economics and Management Sciences* 5(2014): 44-50; K. Mots'oene, "Urbanization and Aging: The Survival of the Aged in an Urbanizing City, Maseru, Lesotho" *Journal of Emerging Trends in Economics and Management Sciences* 5(2014); 316-22.

127   L. Pellerano, M. Moratti, M. Jakobsen, M.Bajgar and V. Barca, *Child Grants Programme Impact Evaluation: Follow Up Report* (Oxford: Oxford Policy Management, 2014).

128   H. Alderman and J. Hoddinott, "Growth-Promoting Social Safety Nets. 2020 Focus Brief on the World's Poor and Hungry People" IFPRI, Washington DC, 2007.

129   http://www.ifpri.org/book-7765/ourwork/researcharea/social-protection

130   Alderman and Hoddinott, "Growth-Promoting Social Safety Nets" p. 1.

131   DSD, SASSA and UNICEF, *The South African Child Support Grant Impact Assessment* (Pretoria, 2012).

132   M. Musi, "The Case of Informal Cross-Border Trade Between Lesotho and Durban, South Africa" MA Thesis, University of Natal, 2002.

Printed in the United States
By Bookmasters